Keep the Drama in Front of the Camera!

Conflict Resolution for Film & Television

Ken Ashdown & Helene Arts

Published by Conflict Resolution for Creatives (CRFC) Press c/o
Fifth House Group
P.O. Box 23006 RPO Sunnycrest
Gibsons, BC, Canada
V0N 1V0
1-844-584-4687
crfc@fifthhousegroup.com

For bulk discounts or to reach the authors for speaking engagements, training, or consultation, please contact the publisher or visit the Fifth House Group website at www.fifthhousegroup.com.

ISBN (paperback): 978-0-9940810-7-0
First edition.
Published January, 2017. Printed in the United States.

10 9 8 7 6 5 4 3 2 1

Cover design by Iryna Spica. Copy Editor: Jennifer D Munro.

DEDICATIONS

Ken:

To my wife, Danika, for her ruthless support and encouragement. And to
the screenwriters, actors, directors, cinematographers, costumers, makeup
people, VFX artists, sparks, grips, sound designers, and the myriad artists,
crafts and business people who work together to create cinematic magic –
thank you for making life that much more entertaining.

Helene:

For my beloveds, Emmanuelle, Ciaran, Aisling and Hanna.
"There is no end. There is no beginning. There is only the infinite passion
of life. "
— Federico Fellini

CONTENTS

ACKNOWLEDGMENTS

Ken:

Throughout my career I have had the great fortune of working with extremely smart and talented people in many sectors of the entertainment industry, and it would take a whole book to thank them all by name. I have been equally blessed in writing this book. I must thank my business partner and coauthor, Helene, for suggesting the collaboration in the first place. Special thanks to Darren Borrowman for inspiring the title. My wife, Danika Dinsmore, is not only the love of my life and a never-ending source of inspiration but also a successful author, screenwriter, poet, educator, and editor whose input was crucial; thanks as always for your ongoing support, love, and encouragement. Once again Jennifer D. Munro was not only lightning fast but also deadly accurate and judicious with her editor's pen. To paraphrase the meme: "All our mistakes are belong to us." As ever, Tod McCoy of Hydra House Press was an invaluable ally and a source of essential e-publishing expertise. I am grateful to my thousands of clients and students, past and present, for gifting me with your presence and for allowing me the honour of serving you. Last but not least, this book would not have been possible without the ongoing support and friendship of the Men's Team: thank you, Dean, Les, David, Leonard, Dieter, and Dan.

Helene:

To all those confused and hurting young people that I worked with as a criminal and young offender mediator; to all those families and children torn apart by pain and dysfunction who came to me as a family mediator; and to all those stressed-out individuals and groups I worked with as a workplace and business conflict resolution consultant: thank you for allowing me to enter onto the sacred ground of your vulnerabilities and emotions. Each time, I honed my skills just a little bit more. Each time, I understood just a little bit more about the human condition. Each time, I saw my own reflection in the mirrors of your situations, and learned. All along my clients, colleagues and students have been my greatest teachers. I am deeply grateful to all of you.

My brilliant co-author Ken Ashdown deserves the bulk of the credit for this book - it came into being in whole part because of his persistence and dedication. He has my ongoing respect and admiration.

Finally, a special thank you to my friend Guillaume Poulin. In sharing his in-depth knowledge and experience of this very special and magical field of creativity and entertainment, he has taught me so much. My appreciation and enjoyment of it is greatly increased thanks to him.

PREFACE

If you're reading this book as a preventive measure and for personal or professional development, congratulations on your proactivity, foresight, and leadership. We strongly believe it will pay dividends for years to come, at least in terms of your peace of mind and perhaps your career trajectory. Depending on your level of industry experience, some of the content in the introductory portion of the book, describing the history and costs of conflict in the business, may seem familiar (perhaps uncomfortably so!), and you can safely skim over it. For relative newcomers, our aim is not to frighten or discourage you, but to provide a realistic view of life in a competitive and occasionally intense industry.

If you're reading it because you're currently embroiled in a conflict, stop right now and turn immediately to the practical, problem-solving skills explained in Part Three: Essential Conflict Prevention and Resolution Skills, starting on page 82. You can come back to the introduction and the more theoretical sections later, once you've got a handle on your current situation.

In either case, make sure you do come back and read the other sections, because they provide valuable context and insight into how conflicts get started in the first place and how they escalate. There you will also learn other important aspects of conflict theory to help you prevent and manage conflicts more effectively over the long term. Note the use of the term "manage," which is an important distinction, because not all conflicts can be resolved, but they can almost certainly be managed. Whether or not you are ultimately responsible for the issue (or the people involved) in your current role, the tools and techniques described herein will allow you to deal with it in a way that will at least limit the physical and emotional energy you might otherwise need to invest in the conflict.

Between them, the authors have worked in the creative industries (including entertainment and high tech) for over thirty years, and, more specifically, we have been developing filmmakers and animators (among other artists and crafts persons) since 2002. In that time, we have witnessed the terrible tolls taken on production teams and individual careers, many of which have been hobbled or effectively ended by conflict. We have worked with hundreds of individuals, organizations, and teams whose workplaces and family members have suffered unnecessarily because of conflict that was either managed poorly or not at all. We have yet to meet anyone working in the field who does not have horror stories to share from working on set or in another area of the film and television business. Every one of them also told us that a book like this one would be a much-needed and welcome resource. We were only too happy to oblige, even if we were dismayed by the necessity of writing it.

We believe that movies and television are not only a reflection of our society but also a strong influence on it, one that is itself informed and shaped by the forces at work during the act of creation. When conflict intrudes, it can impact both the artistic and commercial success of the finished product, and it can have a deeper, more insidious effect on the broader culture. Our goal in writing this book (as with others in the series) is to provide a practical, step-by-step guide to help those in the industry reduce the frequency and intensity of conflicts by addressing the unique ways in which conflict can manifest in the making of filmed entertainment. If the book can help "keep the drama in front of the camera" where it belongs, more entertainment can be produced by happier, less stressed-out people, and then perhaps that positive energy will filter out to the audience and beyond.

WHOM THIS BOOK IS FOR

The entertainment industry is built on relationships. Perhaps more than most businesses, it's not necessarily *what* you know that makes you successful in film or television, so much as *who* you know. Agents, casting directors, writers, producers, directors, studio personnel – all rely on the strength of their connections to get their script into the right hands, to attach talent to a project, to package a project, or to take a pitch meeting. Each production is an ad hoc network organization that comes together for the purpose of creating a specific show or series, only to be disbanded promptly once principal photography is done, and then perhaps reassembled in a different configuration for a future show. The trick is to ensure that you remain among those who consistently get called to work on a show. That requires a minimum standard of professionalism, a sufficiently pleasant personality, and ideally the ability to deal effectively with conflicts if or when they arise. Despite appearances, very few are those who can still land roles despite a history of difficult behaviour, especially in the formative stages of their career.

Unfortunately, the film and television industry also lends itself to friction. It faces a confluence of challenges that is rare in other industries. First, there's the issue of heightened time sensitivity in the production phase. Principal photography on a feature often takes place in as little as fifteen or thirty days, whereas a "long" production schedule may take as many as ninety. On episodic television, that time scale is compressed even further. Relative to businesses that produce consumer products or services on a routine, ongoing basis, this creates unparalleled urgency to resolve conflict situations quickly. In-demand actors or other key creatives may be contractually bound to wrap their work by a hard deadline so they can be free to work on their next scheduled project. The strain of these tight timelines can also contribute to conflict.

Second, and equally pressing, is the financial strain. With every tick of the clock, a tremendous sum of money is potentially wasted if a production is brought to a standstill for any reason. There are enough variables already: exterior shoots are subject to the forces of nature, and weather doesn't always cooperate. Nor do animal actors, or planes flying through local airspace, or a host of other annoyances that can delay production. Multiple takes are par for the course, and technical glitches are usually taken in stride, but interpersonal conflicts are as unpredictable as they are destabilizing. That many are also preventable makes them all the more frustrating.

Third, a professional film or TV set can be strictly hierarchical in a way that many contemporary businesses are not. The rigidity of the pecking order can vary greatly, but, generally, the higher the production budget, the more strictly the hierarchy is maintained. Not entirely without reason, audiovisual production remains very much a vertically oriented, command-and-control type of setup, with most of the power and authority vested in the top tiers (typically the producer and director, as per Figure 1).

Executive Producer (Studio/Network)

Location Manager

Production Manager

Producer

Casting Director

Director

Assistant Director(s)

Director of Photography

Sound Designer

Production Designer

Editor

Assistant Camera

Clapper Loader

Sound Recordist

Art Director

Dubbing Editor

Gaffer

Focus Puller

Boom Operator

Special Effects Producer

Costumes

Best Boy

Grip

Makeup

Sparks

Props

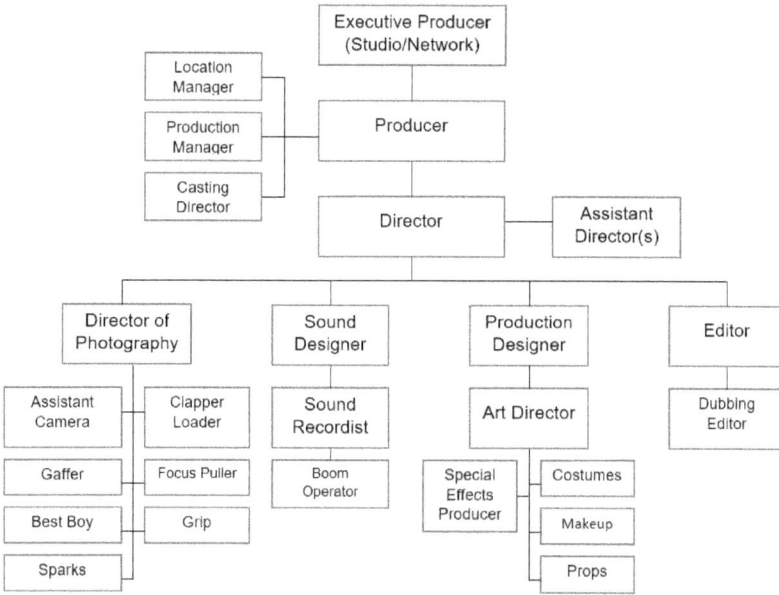

Figure 1: A typical production hierarchy.

This is in contrast to industries other than film and television, where the trend over the last few decades has been to flatten organizations, or at least to make them more matrix-like, allowing for greater cross-functional collaboration, communication, decision-making equality, and accountability.

Finally, there's the complexity of productions that are either unionized, non-unionized, or a blend of union and non-union labour, all of which are subject to their own rules and regulations (or lack thereof), which can vary depending on the jurisdiction in which the production is shooting. And when child actors are involved, studio teachers and health and safety monitors must look after the welfare of any minors in the cast, again depending on the jurisdiction in which filming takes place. Each of these situations requires filmmakers to adhere to an array of confusing and sometimes contradictory set of rules and regulations.

Together these factors make conflict prevention and resolution in the film and television industry that much trickier. In short, there are enough external threats to the industry, like piracy, market fragmentation, and cable TV cord-cutting, without having to worry about internal issues resulting from conflict.

Therefore, we wrote this book for people in every facet of the film and

TV business who deal with these and other challenges, individually or collectively, on a regular basis. This includes both the "creatives" and the so-called "suits" (a questionable distinction that will be tackled in a subsequent work-in-progress). The book is also intended for the agents, financiers, insurers, or anyone else with whom filmmakers might come into contact – including their loved ones. May it be equally useful whether you experience the conflicts directly or indirectly.

Its purpose is to help you, your cast and crew – or your producer, distributor, network exec, publicist, etc. – not only survive conflict relatively unscathed, but also make it work for you wherever possible. As we'll suggest, well-managed conflict can provide a valuable and perhaps necessary contribution to the creative process. It's only when conflict goes unmanaged, or is managed poorly, that it devolves into a destructive force.

Realistically, it's not a matter of *if* conflict will happen, but *when*. Conflict is inevitable, because even the most skilled and willfully independent among us can't work in total isolation forever. Every auteur still needs their crew to bring the vision to the big screen.

You may want or need to read this book if you are experiencing any or all of these issues (simply substitute "cast and crew" or "coworkers" with "significant other" or "family members" if you're not in the biz yourself):

- trouble communicating effectively with cast and crew members
- crew being secretive or withholding information
- frequent groundless arguments and/or displays of insensitivity towards colleagues
- colleagues taking unreasonably rigid positions in disagreements
- unfair or unwarranted criticism directed at one or more crew members
- relations between crew members becoming noticeably frosty or stiff and formal

These are just some of the many symptoms of possible conflict on your set or wherever you might work in the industry. If conflict is present, this book can help you deal with it more effectively and maintain the relationship(s) while reducing your stress and anxiety levels. If you're one of the few lucky ones to have managed to avoid conflict so far, this book will help you keep it that way by applying effective conflict prevention strategies.

Before proceeding, we need to offer a disclaimer. In our consulting work we must assure our clients of the utmost in confidentiality. Aside from some of the well-documented, historical cases presented here, the examples we offer in this book are not based on particular people or incidents and are highly fictionalized. They may be drawn from real-life experience, but they are mostly amalgamations of a variety of situations we have encountered. We have taken liberties with the specifics but have tried to stay as true as possible to the underlying principles, concepts, or causal factors in an effort to present realistic scenarios. In all cases names have been changed to protect identities.

A final word of caution before we begin: It's tempting to dismiss conflict, or at least one person's unwanted behaviour, as the product of "ego." We often hear about a star's or director's egocentricities in the media. Beware of oversimplifications. Like any generalization, labels don't help uncover the real root cause of a conflict or identify possible solutions. They're just another way to objectify people, to dehumanize and see them as "other," which is a good way to prolong or escalate a conflict. In Part Two, where we analyze the roles of feelings, needs, and strategies in conflict, we'll learn what's really behind ostensibly ego-driven behaviour and decode that information to manage or resolve conflict.

A key purpose of this book is to make sure that you can take the necessary steps to minimize the likelihood that a conflict will devolve into a destructive, personal attack, or worse. Even if the other party never learns or utilizes the tools and techniques contained in this book, you can still guide them towards a more satisfactory outcome. You hold the power in your hands.

PICTURE'S UP:
INTRODUCTION

A Brief History of Conflict in Film & TV

If you're reading this, chances are you've already discovered that one of filmmaking's greatest joys is also one of its most frustrating challenges: it is necessarily a collaborative endeavor. There is really no way to avoid working with other people. Even a minimalist, micro-budgeted guerrilla shoot requires a small production team comprising a director, cinematographer, actor, and maybe a boom operator or gaffer. Assuming the writer-director doubles as the editor and director of photography, and if all other participants are wearing multiple, hyphenated hats, there's still no getting around the fact that it's a group effort.

As budgets increase, factor in additional personnel, like producers, assistant directors, production managers, grips, hair and makeup, wardrobe, craft services, and other departments and roles. That's without considering productions with multiple units. By the time we get to visual effects and the titles, a small army of talented collaborators has been assembled. From pre-production to principal photography through to post, the number of creatives involved in a given film or TV show is potentially in the thousands. And then there are studio executives, investors, distributors, marketing and publicity people…. From indie to major, and from Bollywood to Hollywood, there is always potential for conflict in film and television.

As they say in negotiation circles, it takes everyone to say yes and only one person to say no. The happiest and most harmonious of productions can still run the risk of an occasional difficult situation because there will always be differing ideas, perspectives, jobs or roles, goals and objectives, beliefs, opinions, or values, just to name a few of the things about which people can passionately disagree. It's a normal part of human nature. Everyone wants the best for the picture; they just don't always agree on what that means.

The stakes can be high. In the film and TV industry, perhaps more than in any other, time is money. Idle moments on a film or TV set can literally cost tens of thousands of dollars, and with production budgets on studio tent-pole pictures now frequently surpassing the USD $100 million mark, the pressure on all involved can be intense. A "cheap" indie film (by 2016 standards) can still spend five million dollars or more on the basics. That's a lot of pressure, especially when folks are mortgaging their houses or maxing out their credit cards to finance the picture.

We see and hear evidence of conflict in film and television in the tabloids or on TMZ every day, so it might be redundant to delve into a history of conflict in film and TV here. But it's worth remembering that conflict in the business has been with us as long as there has been a moving picture industry, and much of it transpires behind the scenes too. Although the highest profile conflicts tend to involve above-the-line talent, there are often issues within below-the-line departments, or between the writer(s), production designers, or other pre-production collaborators. Our company has worked with postproduction special visual effects houses to resolve issues there too. What, you might ask, can possibly go wrong when artists are silently and intently focused on their computer screens, modeling or texturing CGI animated characters or props? You might be surprised. In our experience, no area is immune to interpersonal problems.

Behind-the-scenes conflict in film and TV comes in many sizes and shapes. Most famous (or infamous) are those struggles occurring between directors and actors while in production. In many cases the former allegedly subject the latter to verbal abuse, excessive repeated takes, and forms of bullying or harassment. A quick Google search for examples of on- and off-set clashes turns up dozens of results. These include Alfred Hitchcock vs. Tippi Hedren in *The Birds*; Stanley Kubrick vs. Shelley Duvall and Scatman Crothers in *The Shining*; David O. Russell vs. George Clooney (during *Three*

Kings), Lily Tomlin (on *I Heart Huckabees*), and James Caan (*Nailed*); Michael Bay vs. Megan Fox in *Transformers*; Sydney Pollack vs. Dustin Hoffman in *Tootsie*; and many, many more. Often these episodes are explained (or justified) retrospectively by the directors as attempts to create a realistic atmosphere or provoke a desired reaction from the actors onscreen. Whether this is truth or self-serving PR spin is a matter of speculation. Either way, people experienced real human emotions – some of them very unpleasant indeed. Some situations might even fall into the category of bullying and harassment, which are at the extreme end of a scale of emotional distress that we'll examine in the theoretical underpinnings of conflict resolution in Part One.

Conflicts aren't confined to directors and actors, of course. There have been instances where screenwriters have clashed with other writers. One of the most fascinating collaborations was the long, successful, but tempestuous relationship between the chalk-and-cheese duo of Billy Wilder and Charles Brackett. Despite their many personal and professional differences – and public feuding – they somehow coauthored many films that were critical or commercial hits, or both. A large percentage of them are now regarded as all-time classics, such as *Sunset Boulevard*, *Ninotchka*, and *The Lost Weekend*. It may be hard to believe that the late, great comic actor Garry Shandling was anything other than universally loved, at least judging by the tributes that poured in following his untimely passing in early 2016. But his writing partner on *It's Garry Shandling's Show*, Alan Zweibel, told Variety that the relationship "was not easy. In fact, after our show ended, we were hardly speaking — the unfortunate result of two strong personalities growing resentful of the same traits that drew them together in the first place."[1] Eventually, after years of not talking to each other, Shandling and Zweibel patched things up, but it demonstrates that even some of the most generous and esteemed colleagues can fall prey to conflict.

Actors have warred with fellow actors over the years. An equally long-running (and very public) alleged feud took place over many years between Bette Davis and Joan Crawford, although there is some question whether some of it was manufactured for the benefit of the media (and, ultimately,

---

[1] http://variety.com/2016/tv/news/garry-shandling-dead-alan-zweibel-tribute-1201740577/ , accessed November 26, 2016

the careers of the stars themselves). There were reports of tension manifesting between co-stars Sarah Jessica Parker and Kim Cattrall on the set of *Sex and the City 2*, and battles between Debra Winger and Shirley MacLaine on *Terms of Endearment*. As this is being written, Vin Diesel and Dwayne "The Rock" Johnson are making headlines with some sort of feud on the set of the eighth instalment of the *Fast & Furious* franchise. Tantrums by movie stars are legend; in the Internet era, it's hard to ignore outtakes that go viral on YouTube or Facebook after a star goes ballistic. You're probably thinking of at least one or two famous episodes right now. Exactly why these happen is sometimes hard to ascertain, but they still do, despite ever-present public scrutiny.

Conflict is not limited to the creatives, especially when art intersects with commerce. Money can be an emotionally charged topic, and arguments between directors and their producers, or directors and studio executives, are legion. Director Terry Gilliam took on Universal Pictures over *Brazil*, going so far as to take out a full-page ad in the press to take the studio to task over the release of the film. Richard Donner fought Warner Bros. and producers Alexander and Ilya Salkind over *Superman II*. Other well-documented examples include Orson Welles vs. Universal over *Touch of Evil*; Francis Ford Coppola vs. Paramount on *The Godfather*; and Kevin Reynolds vs. Universal over the trouble-plagued *Waterworld*.

All of these make for sensational reading in the press or online. A more nuanced and revealing perspective can sometimes be had by watching movies about movie-making; at a meta level, these films often provide rare insight into the behind-the-scenes filmmaking challenges. *Lost in La Mancha*, for example, tells the story of director Gilliam's ill-fated retelling of the Don Quixote story, which was marred by many issues including interpersonal conflict. Likewise, *Hearts of Darkness: A Filmmaker's Apocalypse* is a documentary about the many struggles involved in the making of Coppola's classic *Apocalypse Now*, as told by his wife, filmmaker and writer/artist Eleanor Coppola. In it, conflict both on and off the set was an occasional feature. *Lost Soul: The Doomed Journey of Richard Stanley's Island of Dr. Moreau*, on the other hand, chronicles the slow-motion train wreck of a film constantly beset with conflicts. Werner Herzog's *My Best Friend* is another fascinating documentary, about the director's often strained but highly successful relationship with actor Klaus Kinski, which nearly ended in violence on the set of the critically acclaimed *Fitzcarraldo*. No doubt you may have your own favorites to add to this list, and we invite your submissions (you can join the conversation online at www.facebook.com/KeepTheDramaInFrontOfTheCamera).

While this book focuses on interpersonal issues, labour-management disputes are another common manifestation of conflict in the industry. Given the significant number, size, and power of the various unions and guilds in the industry, there is potential for large-scale disruption. Nearly a century ago, in 1919, some of the biggest stars of the day, including D.W. Griffith, Charlie Chaplin, Mary Pickford, and Douglas Fairbanks, founded their own United Artists studio in order to free themselves from the perceived tyranny of the major Hollywood studios. The resulting shift in the traditional power dynamic can still be felt in the industry today. Lengthy strikes by members of the Writers Guild of America in 1988 and 2007-8 wound up costing the industry – and the local Los Angeles economy – hundreds of millions of dollars in lost wages, taxes, and revenues. Issues in the latter dispute included DVD residuals and payments for new media, such as Internet reuse and transmission. As both the technology and business continue to evolve, so will the opportunities for disagreement.

Of the many changes in technology that have impacted the industry over the years, some have resulted in the elimination of traditional roles in film and TV. This has caused discord of its own, and the removal of entire layers of workers hasn't necessarily made navigating working relationships any easier. New skill sets, processes, and people have simply replaced the ones that have been removed. The one skill set that hasn't gone the way of the dodo – and never will, as long as there are human beings who need to live and work together – is the ability to prevent and manage conflict effectively.

The Good News: What We Get from Film & TV

Film and television play a vital role in our economy and in our culture. It's a multi-billion-dollar industry that employs hundreds of thousands around the world in production, distribution, and exhibition. Movies can make us laugh, cry, or think, sometimes all in the course of the same two hours. They can inspire us. They provide an affordable means of escape when times are tough (given historical viewing patterns, the movies are said to be a recession-proof industry). Movies and TV can express our greatest hopes and fears, our dreams and anxieties, our triumphs and our tragedies. Documentaries can be powerful catalysts for change and a force for social justice. Great audiovisual entertainment can bring people together in a way that sports, with its competitive and often nationalistic nature, simply can't.

Clearly, few of the productions cited earlier have suffered noticeably at the box office, either as a direct or indirect result of conflict. For all those that have been negatively affected, either financially or creatively (or both), the shows that do manage to overcome internal problems have no doubt benefited from effective conflict resolution, with the creative chemistry repaired or even enhanced. And not every collaboration is rife with issues. Joe Weisberg and Joel Fields, the showrunners (writer-producers) behind the multiple Emmy-nominated FX spy series *The Americans*, have a congenial and highly functional collaboration, even though their pairing was originally the result of a sort of arranged marriage, thanks to the network and studio. The success of their working relationship is perhaps because the two purposefully sat down and laid the groundwork for their partnership beforehand. As we'll discuss later in Part Two, negotiating the terms of any collaboration – including (or especially) the behaviours, norms, and role expectations, and not just the financial or legal aspects – is always a good idea before proceeding too far down the road.

Even when conflict does exist on a production, it can actually be a positive, productive force for creativity – provided it's managed well, of course. A growing body of research suggests that it's easier to rally teams around a particular decision or motivate them in a given direction when that choice has been hard-fought and won through vigorous debate, dialogue, and discussion. That's because those involved feel more confident that the winning idea has been truly battle-tested, examined from all angles, and agreed upon to be the most robust solution, precisely because it's been subjected to such intense scrutiny. We call this "productive conflict" because the end result is positive and creative. So despite the bleak picture you may have drawn from reading up to this point, the news is not all negative. There is much to appreciate about film and television when it comes to conflict and how it's handled.

The Bad News: What We Don't Get from Film & TV

For all the benefits they bring to the world, film and television do us a tremendous disservice. Set aside, for the moment, the controversies surrounding diversity (or the lack thereof), sexism, and ageism in the industry. Never mind the stylized violence and gore, the gratuitous sex (and sexual objectification of women), the endless remakes and reboots, or other complaints commonly expressed about the content of movies. Ignore the fact that (in Hollywood pictures, at least) all the characters have perfect teeth, or the hero almost always gets the girl in the end. There is another pervasive and more insidious reason that movies and television create unrealistic audience expectations, and it has to do with one of the first rules of storytelling every filmmaker learns in school: *Show, don't tell.*

It's only natural, because film is a visual language, that we let the camera do the talking. For economy's sake, audiences always join the action *in medias res*; very little back story is told, and it's usually limited to quick vignettes. There is always a direct cause-and-effect relationship onscreen; what you see is what you get, and A inevitably leads to B. The audience can only understand the character's intentions and motivations based on what unfolds onscreen. The problem is that the audience only ever sees things from the protagonist's point of view, because of course the goal is to sympathize with him or her. Sometimes there's exposition – for example, when the evil villain patiently explains his diabolical plan to the hero just at the big dramatic climax. Or there may be the occasional flashback or some other clichéd plot device to help the audience understand something that's happened offscreen, or to provide insight into a character's psychological makeup. But we seldom get much insight into any character's mind or motives other than the lead's, and we certainly don't get much of that in real life either.

Even when the camera is omniscient, offering the audience a more all-encompassing view, we still get a simplified picture of reality, one that often relies on stereotypes. In the classic westerns, the villain always wears the black hat. Life is seldom as neat and clean as movies would have us believe; it's usually a lot more nuanced than films or TV shows could ever be. Real people, in particular, are much more multidimensional than the characters are usually portrayed onscreen. Few are purely virtuous or purely evil, and most of us are somewhere in between.

So we have two main issues:

First, *we can't always accept everything at face value.* Things aren't always what they seem. Despite what the movies teach us, reality is infinitely more complex. Just because we feel hurt by something another person might say or do, it doesn't mean they necessarily meant to hurt us; it just feels that way. We have to stop assuming we know what the other person is or was thinking or feeling based solely on what our limited perceptions tell us.

Theory of mind, a concept which is crucial to movie-making, is the notion that human beings can at least imagine what other people are thinking or feeling in a given situation. We might be able to put ourselves in their shoes, but we can't know for sure what's going on in their heads unless we ask, and we get an honest, accurate response. Instead we tend to rely on our assumptions. Someone who laughs, cries, or lashes out at another person onscreen usually does so in direct response to the action immediately preceding it. Real life doesn't always work like that. Another person's laughter, tears, or anger may have nothing to do with us; we might simply be in the right place at the wrong time. Maybe they were recently fired from their job, or broke up with their significant other, or just remembered a funny joke. We don't always get the benefit of exposition, or a flashback that helps us connect the original inciting incident to the reaction. We never get to see everything going on behind the scenes but we still think we get the full picture. Needless to say, our faulty assumptions are a major contributing factor in conflict.

Second, *there's more than one side to any story*. We're raised on the classic fairy tale paradigm that every movie has a clear hero, a victim, and villain. Sometimes the hero is also the victim, or vice versa, but these three roles are represented in every story. If one character is the protagonist, it follows that the other must naturally be the antagonist. In the movies, the latter can sometimes take the form of aliens, or robots, or Mother Nature, but it's always clear who the Bad Guy is. You already know it's never the main character. So when we find ourselves in conflict, we tend to adopt the paradigm and cast ourselves as the avenging hero because we're the main character in our own lives. That means the other person is automatically cast as the villain of the story. If both parties to a conflict filmed their own versions of the story, we'd have two very different movies told from two perspectives, with both casting the other as the bad guy and themselves as the hero or the victim. Both of these contain truth, and neither do.

The Costs of Conflict

You know that a single minute wasted on a film or TV production can mean hundreds, perhaps thousands, of dollars lost. When there's a dispute or a blow-up on set, the producer (or production manager, or AD) typically springs into action to try to resolve matters while the clock is ticking. These surprisingly commonplace events add up and eventually fall to the production and/or studio's bottom line.

Intractable union-management labour relations can be very expensive too. In 1988, the longest strike ever by the film and TV unions and guilds lasted nearly six months. In that time the U.S. entertainment industry was estimated to have lost the equivalent of half a billion dollars in opportunity costs, and while reports of the strike's cost to the larger Los Angeles economy varied, the National Public Radio (NPR) network set the loss at around $1.5 billion.

The business has had its share of major lawsuits filed as a result of mismanaged or unmanaged conflict. Some of the more sensational cases involve outright harassment, which is technically not conflict *per se* but generates extreme levels of pain and suffering, as we'll explain in Part One. It's also terribly expensive. Ample evidence is found in situations such as the Fox News sexual harassment scandal, which is still unraveling as this is written. Even as the story develops, the price tag keeps climbing; some estimates of the network's total settlements already top the $100 million mark. Allegations are still being made about the cable outlet's toxic corporate culture, so the amount could increase substantially before the dust settles.[2]

For every on-set or courtroom battle we hear about in the press, there are probably dozens more being fought that we never learn about because they take place away from the spotlight or under a nondisclosure agreement (NDA). The litigants may fear harm to their reputations if details are made public; they choose to settle out of court; or the parties aren't as high profile or newsworthy. Either way, there are many reasons why it can be hard to determine the true costs of conflict. The invisible, interpersonal issues that can plague individuals, creative teams, and workplaces are hard

---

[2] http://www.latimes.com/entertainment/envelope/cotown/la-et-ct-ailes-settlement-20160906-snap-story.html, accessed November 29, 2016.

to count, and their costs are harder still to estimate accurately. Those day-to-day conflicts that are poorly handled (or completely unmanaged) could be just as expensive in the long run as the lawsuits, perhaps more. Though their costs are not as obvious, nor as easy to assess, they nonetheless take a heavy toll on the industry and its people.

Consider absences due to stress and related health issues. Studios, production companies, crews, actors and agents—to name a few major categories of those affected—all suffer to varying degrees from absenteeism, a significant amount of which can be attributed either directly or indirectly to conflict in the workplace. One individual's unwillingness or inability to deal with another at work might cause them to call in sick just to avoid the conflict. Or the absence might be the result of physical symptoms such as headaches, nausea, or other stress-related illness or injury. Anxiety and sickness have knock-on effects, because they also impact the coworkers of those who are ill or incapacitated, due to the stress of conflict. They may need to cover for the absent colleague, taking on extra responsibilities, which can then result in even more stress and anxiety.

Drug and alcohol abuse, common causes of absenteeism, may themselves be symptoms of conflict. Some people get high as a way to escape or dull the pain, and avoid having to deal with the reality of conflict. Thus we can also factor in the cost of treatments for addiction and the side effects of substance abuse.

The expense of counselling to help overcome the fear and anxiety attached to a particular workplace conflict can be prohibitive, as can the cost of treating the physical symptoms of stress and anxiety as outlined above. Medical care, prescriptions, and physiotherapy all add up, whether the costs are covered by the individual or borne by an insurer.

Confusion or disruption of roles may not incur a direct financial cost, but can result in indirect losses. Affected team or department members might relinquish certain duties, tasks, or activities (either formally or informally) if they tend to lead to conflict. This may be less of an issue on large sets where the roles are highly specialized, clearly defined, and critically interdependent, but it could be a significant problem for smaller indie productions where creatives are wearing multiple hats. It is virtually guaranteed to happen in larger organizations such as studios, unions or guilds, agencies, and so on. Some conflicts might result in individuals being denied voting rights, or other power or privileges. Again, these actions might be formally imposed or they might be covertly initiated by the other party (or parties) to the conflict.

Also at risk in conflict involving creatives is the quality of the work itself. On occasion, it may even be actively sabotaged or destroyed out of anger or frustration. Even though nothing ultimately came of it, extra security precautions were taken, at concomitant expense, to ensure that the set, cast, and crew of *The Island of Doctor Moreau* would be protected when Richard Stanley was released from directorial duties on the ill-fated production.[3] A show beset by conflict may experience reduced productivity when it saps the cast and crew's vital physical or emotional energy. There's already enough hurry-up-and-wait fatigue on a typical film set without wasting further writing, rehearsal, shooting, or editing time due to conflict.

Not surprisingly, creative collaborations inevitably find their output diminished in all sorts of ways when faced with conflict. In addition to draining physical resources, conflict can impact artistic input. It can lead to the withholding of creative ideas, especially if someone fears conflict potentially arising from their contributions. Affected individuals might keep their best ideas to themselves and reserve them for future use if they believe they aren't getting a fair hearing in the current situation. It's hard to be focused, and loyal, when you've always got one eye on the door. Idea generation suffers, too. Every creative endeavor thrives on original concepts, or at least an interesting, original twist. But conflict can lead to unproductive or inefficient brainstorming when fear of judgment or censorship – by oneself or others – is rampant. These are just a few of the many ways creativity itself can suffer.

Even assuming good, creative input can be generated and shared in the midst of conflict, the quality of decisions may still be at risk. Inferior choices are often made in haste just to "get it over with" and stop the bickering. Or they may be made while one or more persons' ideas are being withheld. In either case, the resulting decisions are bound to be short-lived, or subject to second-guessing. Equally questionable are those decisions made by one faction "ganging up" on another.

It's worth noting that when managed productively, conflict can actually

---

[3] For a fascinating peek behind the scenes at the making of the troubled project, see the aforementioned *Lost Soul: The Doomed Journey of Richard Stanley's Island of Dr. Moreau*, the 2014 documentary by David Gregory.

be crucial to getting the best quality decisions out of any group or team. We'll examine the idea of healthy and productive conflict in due course. (For a wonderful primer on the subject, we recommend former BBC executive and film and television producer Margaret Heffernan's TED Talk entitled "Dare to disagree."[4])

Meanwhile there are other dollars-and-cents costs to take into account where conflict is concerned. Replacement of personnel and the orientation of new hires is another significant expense. Recruitment, "on-boarding," and training new hires all incur significant hard costs, over and above the lost momentum and productivity. Human Resources professionals can attest that it's one of the most expensive HR processes undertaken by any organization, especially when new recruits don't survive the probationary period. In those cases, the cycle simply repeats, and the costs mount. It takes time, effort, and patience to find and acclimate a new hire with just the right fit for the team, department, or organization. It's often an unnecessary and entirely avoidable cost.

Looking further afield, there are social costs to conflict. The damage to relationships at home, in the community, or in the industry can be significant, if not easily tallied. Conflicts might originate inside the production, team, or organization, but they have a tendency of "leaking" out into other domains. Those affected may bring the stress and frustration of work home with them at the end of the day, where it manifests in family conflict. We call this the "wallpaper bubble effect," and if you've ever tried to lay wallpaper, you know how it works: suppressing an air bubble under the wallpaper in one area only causes it to pop up elsewhere. A similar thing happens with anger or other emotions suppressed in a conflict; it's hard to keep them from manifesting in other areas, including one's primary/romantic relationship, at home, or in the community.

Tarnished reputations are a heavy price to pay for those in conflict. The film and TV business may employ thousands around the world, but it's still a fairly closed shop. It's no coincidence that the game "Six Degrees of Kevin Bacon" is based on the notion that everyone knows everyone else through one or more contacts. Word gets around the grapevine quickly. Cast, crew, or employees that have a history of conflict don't make good candidates for the next gig. That said, the industry does seem to have a

---

[4] http://www.ted.com/talks/margaret_heffernan_dare_to_disagree

surprisingly high tolerance for some individuals connected to a disproportionate share of conflicts. We probably all know of some "marquee" talent whose name recognition value tends to give them a pass for bad behaviour. For this reason, conflict may affect the lesser known lights more severely, but it catches up with everyone eventually.

We were somewhat surprised to learn, for example, that one hotly tipped young director straight out of film school left a trail of bitter cast and crew members after his debut studio production, and was subsequently hired to helm a TV series. The world-class crew on that first feature had rallied around him in support, knowing that he would be under tremendous pressure, but he quickly squandered that goodwill with his dictatorial style and confrontational approach. Regardless of why his TV series was greenlit after his early, unwelcome behaviour, the director will have a progressively smaller pool of experienced, professional talent to work with if this pattern continues.

In general, if not (yet) in this particular case, recurring destructive conflict signals that a person or organization is probably tough to work with. In a buyer's market, it's easier to bypass "difficult" actors or directors, etc., in favour of others that can either manage or resolve conflicts effectively. Thus, career limitation or failure is another by-product of conflict. A long history of conflicts can make it hard to get another job, but even a single, unresolved issue can limit one's choices if the conflict is sufficiently severe. This might seem unlikely in the film business, where megastars can wield tremendous box office (and negotiating) power, but it happens. Companies with "revolving door syndrome" due to frequent personnel changes can also find it very difficult to attract or retain new employees, for similar reasons.

The loss of a single creative talent can be catastrophic. It's bad enough in the music business; for every band like the Beatles, whose individual members go on to lucrative solo careers post-breakup, or the Rolling Stones, who have survived the replacement of several members over the years, there are countless others who struggle to recapture a fraction of their former financial or artistic glory. In the movie business, which is inherently a collaborative effort, the loss of a single creative participant can likewise portend disaster. This is because – and not despite – the fact that we are more interdependent.

As the famous case of writer-director Billy Wilder and cowriter Charles

20

Beckett illustrates, a team split can destroy the creative partnership's unique chemistry. Theirs was just one collective genius that was effectively silenced when they were unable to work out their differences. With the end of their collaboration the pair seemed to lose the ability to make equivalent artistic and box office magic. As so often happens with genuine creative synergies, the whole proved to be greater than the sum of its parts. Such losses are felt at many levels, from the individuals involved to the studios that hire them.

Then there are the disappointed audiences. There's only so much discord, or creative patchiness, that even the most rabid fan will tolerate from any studio, production company, or creative team. Eventually the conflict will start to impact their moviegoing experience. Real life will intrude, overshadowing the creative content. Fans move on and find other artists or franchises to follow, whether or not the team behind them actually breaks up. If the creative output suffers as a result of conflict, that's one more reason fans might abandon a favorite series. The same is true for organizations: customers and clients will find another firm to do business with if the conflict trickles down to affect the quality of their product or service.

If left to fester, a situation will inevitably deteriorate, and when all civility breaks down, personal safety and security can be another casualty of conflict. Violence is not unknown in the industry, and it can happen on set as well as off.

By now we hope you are convinced that unresolved or poorly managed conflict will cost you significant money, time, relationships, reputation, and perhaps rob the world of some classic shows. It doesn't have to be this way. If you deal with conflict the moment you suspect a problem – or better yet, if you learn how to take preventive measures and reduce the likelihood of eruptions in the first place – you dramatically increase the chances that matters will be resolved successfully. This means that the situation won't get worse, you will save yourself lots of stress and anxiety, and the creativity will continue, if not flourish.

Another critical thing will happen when conflict is dealt with proactively: your fellow filmmakers (and those who live or work with them) will learn from the experience and grow. On a personal level, you will improve your conflict prevention and management skills. Like any other skill, conflict resolution gets better with practice. Eventually you will develop a reputation for your leadership skills, and for being a pleasant professional collaborator. Given the choice of working with a production assistant, grip, or gaffer with strong technical knowledge but no people skills and one with less than complete knowledge but plenty of leadership skills, most people would prefer the latter. Who doesn't want more opportunities?

Now you know why you will want to address conflict as soon as you realize something is amiss: the costs of not doing so are obvious and far too high. The personal, professional, and monetary risks are simply not worth it.

Our first priority, therefore, is to identify the underlying causes of conflict, and some of the signs that indicate it is time to act.

PART ONE:
BASIC CONFLICT RESOLUTION THEORY

Learning outcomes: By the end of this section, you should have the skills, knowledge, and attitudes necessary to

- distinguish between disagreement, conflict, and harassment/bullying;
- interpret conflict as a signal that something needs to change;
- recognize four warning signs of conflict (Emotional, Physical, Behavioural, and Relational);
- determine when it's appropriate to get help managing or resolving a conflict;
- assess and evaluate a conflict situation;
- distinguish between the types of conflict resolution assistance available; and
- locate a variety of resources available for assistance with conflict resolution.

The Difference Between Disagreement, Conflict,

and Bullying/Harassment

There are three terms that people tend to use interchangeably: disagreement, conflict, and harassment, and sometimes bullying (which is a form of harassment). Depending on how emotionally charged you are, you might use any one of these words to describe the current state of affairs. But it's important to make a distinction, because the meaning of these terms will make a difference in how to deal with each situation most effectively.

To clarify these terms, we can place disagreement, conflict, and harassment on a continuum of pain or emotional distress, like the one in Figure 2:

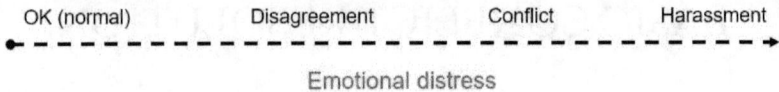

OK (normal)	Disagreement	Conflict	Harassment

Emotional distress

Figure 2: The conflict continuum.

As we move from left to right along this continuum, the feelings get progressively more intense. It's important to note that this is not a time line: situations that are normal or OK don't necessarily become disagreements over time, disagreements don't always become conflict, and conflict doesn't eventually turn into harassment one hundred percent of the time. Of course this can and does happen, but only under certain conditions, which we'll explain in due course. Remember, it's a continuum of *emotional discomfort*, which means that a disagreement can be uncomfortable, but it doesn't feel anywhere near as upsetting as actual conflict does. Even the latter's very unpleasant feelings don't compare to harassment or bullying, when people can experience a profound sense of violation and/or fear, extreme powerlessness, and other unpleasant emotions.

The reason it's important to be able to differentiate between these states is because if you understand what has to happen in order for one state to lead to the next, then you can use that knowledge to prevent the current situation from devolving into something worse. If a disagreement is not handled well, or at all, it can escalate into conflict, and a conflict that remains unresolved has the potential to turn into a harassment situation. Clearly, neither is desirable, but both outcomes are within your power to prevent.

On the far left of the continuum, when everything is OK between people (i.e., a normal, non-conflicted state), there is no problem with the relationship: conversations carry on as normal, and the level of emotional distress is at zero. When issues do arise, such as a tough decision, you usually try to work them out as soon as you can. It isn't always easy or fun, but you try. If in the process of addressing the problem you find yourselves stuck but still fundamentally getting along, then that's a disagreement. You might differ on an issue, but fundamentally the relationship is intact. The people involved may not see eye to eye, but they still like, trust, and respect each other. As the cliché goes, you simply agree to disagree. It's nothing personal, just a difference of opinion, so there is very little (if any) emotional "heat" around the issue.

Conflict is a different, intensified state: You are in disagreement, but there is also something that has happened between you and the person(s) with whom you disagree. Depending on how serious that something is, your relationship has probably sustained damage; words have been exchanged that leave one or more of you hurting and feeling negatively towards each other. Trust is weakened. Respect is faltering. The situation has become personal, and emotions are running high(er). Commonly heard at the conflict stage include such familiar lines as these:

- "You betrayed me,"
- "You've ruined things,"
- "Obviously you don't care,"
- "You never listen,"
- "You do this all the time,"
- "I don't give a shit anymore,"
- "I'm getting sick of this,"
- "I'm so pissed off/hurt/disappointed/frustrated," etc.

Conflict is a stronger emotional state than disagreement, so it rates higher on the continuum of emotional distress.

It's important to distinguish here between dysfunctional, or *destructive*, conflict, and *productive* conflict (yes, there is such a thing!). The former is exactly what you might expect based on the name: it means individuals aren't cooperating or collaborating well, teams aren't functioning properly, and things are probably falling apart. Productive conflict, on the other hand, is that which ultimately brings with it positive outcomes – assuming, of course, it never reaches the destructive stage, or, if it does, the situation can be salvaged.

The paradox of productive conflict is that teams, groups, or organizations that survive it often go on to be much more healthy and high-functioning, with trust levels even stronger than prior to the conflict. In the academic literature, group cohesion is positively correlated with team or group performance, and conflict resolution is positively correlated with group cohesion. In other words, the research indicates that productive conflict, and/or successful conflict resolution where dysfunctional conflict has occurred, likely contributes to better team, group, or organizational outcomes.

A more in-depth discussion of this phenomenon is beyond the scope of this book, but the key is to understand that conflict *per se* is not necessarily bad, and it can in fact make a production or company even better if used consciously and managed well. The cohesiveness and trust are improved precisely because work has been done to surface previously unseen issues, feelings, and needs, and to resolve the situation effectively. This is not unlike some troubled marriages that go on to be even stronger and more loving if they can weather the occasional storms, perhaps undergoing counselling to improve communication and ensure the partners' mutual care-taking.

Productive conflict also means that the best and most robust ideas or solutions to common creative challenges will emerge triumphant after lots of thorough examination, analysis, discussion, and even passionate debate. Such decisions are likelier to stick because the participants feel confident that all viewpoints have been heard, taken into account, weighed, and rigorously tested.

Harassment, like its variant *bullying*, takes conflict to a whole new (and more dangerous) level. Note that there doesn't need to be a preexisting conflict, nor need there have been an initial disagreement between the parties. Instead, someone might have exhibited a behaviour that another finds offensive — for example, persistent jokes at someone else's expense — and despite asking them several times to stop, the offensive behaviour continues. Perhaps one party is using social media to deliberately humiliate or intentionally sabotage another's reputation. Maybe someone has some secret information and is using that power to intimidate. Or it might be that someone has acted contrary to a law or policy, as is the case with discrimination or unwanted sexual advances.

Regardless of the specifics, harassment can be defined as some sort of violation of a person's basic human rights and dignity. If you are dealing with a situation at the harassment level, then please get help from someone with experience in this area who can give you the advice and support that you need. This person may be a professional of some kind or a wise and trusted friend or colleague — whatever works for you — but do get that help. (We'll cover when to get help, what kind to get, and where to get it, later in Part One.)

Returning to our continuum of emotional distress, you can see how each one of these states, from normal/OK through harassment/bullying, feels quite different, and each of these terms means something just as distinct.

Now that you know the terminology and the basic differences between these states, you have just increased your awareness of how to prevent a situation from deteriorating. In short, if you find yourself in a disagreement with someone, keep focused on the issue — that is, the problem that needs to be fixed. It's never the person that needs to be fixed, no matter how much they may frustrate you – it's their *behaviour* that needs to be fixed. The problem is not the individual themself, no matter how irritated or upset you feel, or how persistently you feel it. It's *what they're saying or doing* that can be changed, whereas people seldom change all that much without a lot of effort and sheer will. So never let it become personal! Avoid shifting the focus from what, to who. Once the parties begin talking about what's wrong with each other, instead of discussing the reason for the original disagreement central to the conflict, they have just made things worse and much harder to resolve. The term for this is *conflict escalation.*

If preventing a situation from becoming personal sounds easier said than done, the subsequent sections of this book will give you many valuable tools and techniques you need to deal with disagreements more effectively when they arise. You will learn to keep disagreements from becoming personal and to prevent disagreements from escalating into conflicts. You will learn basic techniques and skills for resolving many different types of conflict and keeping most any situation from spiraling out of control.

Conflict: A Signal That Something Needs to Change

We have just differentiated between a number of relationship states according to their emotional intensity, or levels of pain and suffering, from normal to harassment or bullying. But what is conflict, anyway, and what makes it harder to deal with than mere disagreement?

Conflict is a word we see or hear all too frequently in the news, but tend not to think about too deeply. But it's important to understand, because it can shape our attitude towards it and, ultimately, how we choose to deal with it.

Ironically, there is no universal definition of conflict. There are many definitions in encyclopedias and countless books on conflict but very little (if any) agreement about a single meaning. So we are going to define it thus:

Conflict is simply *a signal that something needs to change.*

To be more explicit, it's a signal that something needs to change, either in the relationship between individuals, or in a given situation, or both.

By defining it this way, we have two aims: first, to take some of the emotional heat out of the term. People fear conflict, often with good reason. In the context of the daily news, we associate it with its extreme forms, like violence or war, and the terrible costs they inflict. But it can actually have a more benign – even beneficial – connotation. As we'll soon learn, some conflict can actually be good for you and your creativity. So it's critical to avoid letting the word cause undue anxiety, control you, or cause you to avoid conflict. (Besides, good storytellers understand that a character must experience some form of conflict in order to grow.)

Our second goal with this definition is to let you know that there is hope in conflict, and it doesn't necessarily result in negative outcomes. On the contrary, it simply lets you know that something needs to be fixed before you can move on. Handled well, that shift can provide a positive and energizing basis for longer-lasting, more satisfying creative collaborations. To use a film analogy, just because the lighting was off, someone missed their mark, or an ad-libbed line didn't work, doesn't mean you have to throw out the entire day's shoot: a slight adjustment and a re-take is all you need to be able to move forward and have a better final product.

Furthermore, the mere presence of a conflict doesn't tell the whole story. It's often a symptom of something else. The bigger picture includes the back story, how the characters got to this point, and (dramatically speaking) the inciting incident that led to the current conflict. Somewhere along the way, something has gone wrong between the figures in the story, or with the situation they are in, and now they find themselves in conflict. Something needs to change or the conflict will continue and maybe worsen. That's all. You can look upon it as an opportunity.

In film and television, the audience always joins the story *in medias res*, i.e., in the midst of the action. A lot is unseen, left up to the imagination. Filmmakers rely on this cinematic shorthand, and audiences intuitively understand it. But in reality conflicts don't happen that spontaneously or in a vacuum; they develop. The luxury we have with our entertainment is that we can assume the audience fills in the blanks, connects the dots, and makes the causal connections. Clever editing can do that. We seldom have that luxury offscreen. Instead, we need to ask the right questions about where the conflict originated, and how. What were the factors that led up to the conflict? What preceded it? These are things we don't always get to see, or at least don't recognize when they're presented.

The fact that people have ended up in a conflict only tells you that something went off the rails between them somewhere along the line. What we still need to identify is exactly what it is that derailed their interaction. In this industry, there are as many possible causes of conflict as there are people and situations. Issues could arise as a result of any one, or combination, of how the following things are handled:

- creative differences
- decision-making
- talking about difficult subjects
- collaborating
- dealing with each other as people and as professionals
- reactions to common triggers, such as control, respect, etc.

As long as any of these things needs to change in some way before the relationship can be restored to its normal "OK" state, we have a conflict. If there was a simple disagreement and nothing needed to change, then there would be no conflict – that is, no signal. Because that's all it is, just a sign that one or more of these things needs to shift before we can return to normal. We need to address something about the way the relationship, or the situation, has been handled. There's really nothing to fear. The situation is not fatal. The time to worry is when conflict goes unmanaged and escalates.

So how do we know when we're in a conflict? If so much happens behind the scenes in a conflict situation, how can we tell if we need to exercise our conflict prevention or resolution skills? Just as conflict reliably signifies the need for change in a relationship or situation, four universal warning signs alert us to the presence of conflict itself.

Four Warning Signs of Conflict: Emotional, Physical, Behavioural, and Relational

The first crucial step in resolving, or at least managing, conflict is simply to recognize when it may be occurring. As Lucy famously said to Charlie Brown in *A Charlie Brown Christmas*, "The mere fact that you realize you have a problem indicates you are probably not too far gone." The earlier you can detect the signs of an emerging conflict, the sooner you can take steps to resolve or manage it effectively and prevent further harm.

This may sound obvious, but it's far easier to become engulfed in a conflict than it is to identify it. This is probably due to our brain structures, in which the emotional center (the amygdala) is activated well before the cognitive, thinking part of our brain (the cerebral cortex). We'll return to the brain's role in conflict shortly, but the conscious awareness is key: recognizing these four warning signs in a timely manner provides critical insight into what's happening with you personally, beginning with your own emotional state. You can observe what's happening with others (such as fellow cast or crew members) and use your conscious awareness to take appropriate action.

Here we can invoke a useful analogy to film. As in literature, film is full of signposts. If you learn the language of the medium, you'll know what to watch and listen for. Some signs are subtler than others: for example, a long, distant shot can evoke a sense of loneliness or isolation. Moody lighting can signal foreboding and mystery, portending doom. The quickening pace of editing indicates excitement, intensity, or imminent danger. The rhythm and tone of music will dictate whether a scene is suspenseful, lighthearted, or sad. Granted, music can also be used counterintuitively to create an anempathetic effect (think of the scene in *Reservoir Dogs* with Michael Madsen shuffling to Stealers Wheel's "Stuck in the Middle with You"). But in general if enough of these signs are present, the audience will eventually figure out what's going on. Likewise, if you learn to decode the language of conflict, you can have a better understanding of

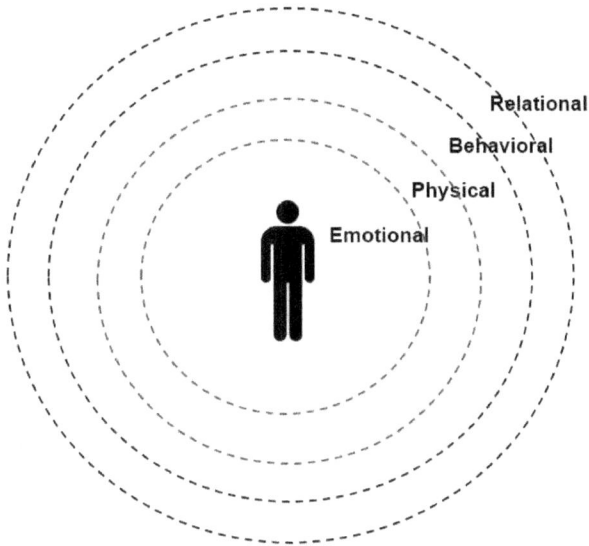

Figure 3: The four warning signs.

what's happening.

The first warning signs that something's wrong with a relationship or situation come from within: these are *emotional signs*. If they go unrecognized or ignored long enough they will eventually spiral outward, manifesting externally as physical warning signs. If the physical indicators are overlooked they will eventually transform into behavioural signs. If these too are left unchecked, they will inevitably result in relational warning signs. This pattern operates as if something (or someone) is trying to tell you something, going to increasing lengths to get your attention. Let's analyze the causes and meanings of these warning signs.

Emotional Signs

The first indicators that something is going amiss for one or more people are internal: their emotions. Your feelings are a reliable barometer, letting you know when things aren't OK. If your normal state is one of comfort, happiness, relaxation, engagement, calm, and/or contentment, then you can usually soon tell when you move away from that baseline. If you tune in, you can usually identify or describe any uncomfortable or unhappy feelings you're having. When trouble is brewing between you and someone else, these are going to be your first indications. Pay attention to them.

Naturally, feelings will vary for each individual involved and according to each situation. For example, one may react to circumstances with sadness while another might be angry or indignant. The same person might even experience different feelings in a similar situation, depending on specifics. (An incident that might seem humorous when it happens to someone else is usually not so funny when it happens to you!) Look no further than the variety of emoticon reactions to any Facebook post for evidence of this (never mind the comments). The intensity of the feeling can also vary from one instance to the next. You might feel confused, frustrated, or overwhelmed if you have multiple feelings simultaneously. The list of possible emotional reactions, or their combinations, is virtually limitless. There is no "right" or "wrong" emotional response; what's most important to remember is that any feeling at all beyond the normal comfort range is a warning.

Figure 4: The feelings VU meter.

As such, feelings should not be ignored or repressed. We may find them easy to downplay because society tends to frown on the expression of unpleasant feelings. Whether or not you choose to divulge them, it's important to recognize that your feelings are a kind of gauge indicating whether or not the person you are dealing with, or the situation you are in, is psychologically healthy or safe. They're like the VU (volume unit) meters on the sound recordist's mixer: when the needles are pushing into the red zone, you know the signal is "clipping" and you need to do something or there will be unwanted noise and distortion. If your emotional VU meter is tipping into the red when you are with a particular person or in a given situation, it's your psyche trying to take care of you. It's sending a red alert, telling you something isn't right and you need to take care of yourself.

Sometimes taking care of yourself means temporarily stepping away from the person or situation causing the discomfort, taking a time-out, and reassessing things. That may be all you need for your emotional barometer to return to its baseline and for you to once again feel calm, relaxed, engaged, happy, or whatever your normal state happens to be. If that's genuinely the case — if after a good night's sleep, the feelings are gone the next morning, and you haven't just repressed or avoided expressing them— then it probably means you don't actually have conflict.

If the feelings persist, however, it could mean there is a problem between you and that other person. Again, we have a tendency to want to

33

ignore unhappy feelings, to mask or avoid dealing with them openly. But they can signal the beginnings of conflict, and therefore it's up to you to deal with the situation. Hoping they'll go away will not help. Trying to "rise above" or "be professional" about the uncomfortable situation are other ways we may cope with unpleasant feelings. But when there is a genuine conflict between two or more people, one in which the relationship is being challenged or damaged in some way, then the feelings are not going to go away on their own. Remember, your emotions serve as a defense mechanism to let you know when a person or situation may not be psychologically healthy and safe for you, and like any other it would be dangerous to disarm or ignore it.

Physical Signs

If the emotional warning signs (i.e., your feelings) are ignored long enough, another natural protective mechanism kicks in. When *physical warning signs* manifest, it's your internal system telling you, in effect, "You didn't pay attention to my earlier alarm, and since my job is to make sure you're all right, I'm going to send you a second set of signals that are harder to ignore."

Again, since everyone is different, people will experience physical warning signs of conflict differently, but some symptoms are quite common. There are the simple and relatively innocuous signs like sweaty palms or a racing heartbeat, indicating anxiety or fear. Other symptoms are more noticeable and worrisome. For example, you may find that you have trouble sleeping. Tossing and turning, waking up at two AM and not being able to fall back asleep again, may be a sign that something is not right. The opposite may also be true: you could begin to sleep more than usual as a way of escaping from the conflict or to help recover from the stress and anxiety it brings. These are two opposite but equally real and valid physical signs of possible conflict. These are harder to ignore than emotions, precisely because they affect not only your mind but your body. You can see them in dilated pupils, goose flesh, or a pale complexion, and feel them in cold, clammy skin – and sometimes, so can others.

Another possible warning sign of conflict is what we will call physical depression, as distinct from emotional or chemical depression. This means you typically find yourself with low energy, dragging your feet throughout the day after hauling yourself out of bed, a pattern that repeats no matter how much quality sleep you get. This is because it takes a lot of physical and emotional energy to cope with the demands of conflict on your body. You might experience an increase in headaches that can be brought on by prolonged stress and anxiety. Other physical indicators of conflict may be activities like smoking, eating, or drinking (at all, or more than usual). Subconscious strategies like these allow us to have physical sensations that mask, albeit temporarily, the other uncomfortable feelings we may be experiencing.

Unfortunately, these physical manifestations have their own knock-on effects, especially when piled on top of the emotional stuff. Consider the consequences of eating, drinking, or smoking to excess, for example. The short-term results may include stomachaches, hangovers, or smoker's cough, and the longer-term consequences can be far more severe, even deadly. Remember, if you have been experiencing any of these physical symptoms, it may mean the original problem hasn't gone away of its own accord, and their purpose is to make the warning more obvious so that you'll finally be moved to do something about it and take care of yourself. Ideally the caretaking will occur before even worse things happen.

Even sleeping too little or too much can have consequences extending beyond the physical. In workplace scenarios, the result of unmanaged conflict is typically an increase in chronic lateness or absenteeism. This brings us to the next set of warning signs, which are behavioural in nature.

Needless to say, any physical symptoms beyond the norm should be discussed with your doctor at the earliest opportunity, especially if they persist. There may be a another, biological reason for their presence. A book cannot possibly be expected to diagnose a problem as accurately or as scientifically as your physician can, and it's imperative to ensure nothing more serious is afoot. Always seek medical care in a timely manner.

Behavioural Signs

If the physical warning signs of conflict go unheeded long enough — that is, if an individual chooses to carry on, not necessarily wallowing in emotional and/or physical misery but avoiding the core issue — then the clever psyche sends another set of signals. This time, the *behavioural* indicators are so overt that they can be observed by other people. It's as if your subconscious is saying, "I'm going to issue another cry for attention, and this time you won't be able to ignore it, because it will show up in a way that others will notice." The logic here is that if you can't (or won't) take care of yourself, you will get someone else to do it for you.

How does your subconscious enlist others in your caretaking? Here, too, everyone is different, but you might recognize some of these more common telltale behaviours:

- A normally calm and serene person begins acting agitated and on edge.
- A typically patient person becomes short-tempered and easily triggered.
- An otherwise engaged and outgoing person begins withdrawing, etc.

Once you learn to spot them, they become harder to miss, especially in other people. You might notice that a crew member who usually goes out socially after the day's wrap starts making excuses to go right home. Someone you normally count on to participate in creative decision-making stops contributing; they may just shrug and say, "Whatever. I don't care." Conversations likewise become more difficult, more tense, more strained. Text or Facebook messages may take much longer to get answered, if they're answered at all—or perhaps the responses are shorter and more tersely worded than usual. Eye contact with others may be avoided, and so on. You don't need to be an expert at conflict resolution to detect them.

Like physical symptoms, these abnormal behaviours could be signs of another issue or problem, but it's a good bet that the thing bothering the person is conflict, especially if the outward behaviour disappears after quitting time. But you won't know for sure unless you ask. Even then, it's possible that they won't respond (at least not immediately or publicly), but generally when someone starts acting outside the norm in terms of what they say, how they say it, or even how much they say, it may be some sort of cry for help. A display of uncharacteristic behaviour will prompt others to ask, "What's going on?" In this sense it's a kind of invitation to assist — not a very articulate or direct one, but a cry for help nonetheless.

Eventually these behaviours are noticed by, and start affecting, other people. Extra work gets taken on in the absence of a meeting participant. Set-ups or shoots are delayed by latecomers. Frustration mounts due to incomplete communication. On and on it goes. As a result, the behaviours also affect the relationship between those involved. This brings us to our fourth, final – and most dramatic – set of conflict warning signs.

Relational Signs

Relational warning signs are, quite simply, those that manifest in the way that people deal with each other. Since these four categories of indicators radiate progressively outward, increasing in their visibility and impact on others, the relational signs are the most difficult of all to ignore. They're the most public and pervasive. Like the other three sets of signals, they also tend to make themselves known if the preceding warning signs go unheeded for too long. And, like the other three, they may also show up differently for everybody, since no two individuals, relationships, or situations are identical.

Still, there are some common relational warning signs. A person feeling uncomfortable or in conflict may avoid others, namely the person(s) with whom they are in conflict. In an office setting, this might mean he or she takes a different route to the cafeteria or the washroom in order to bypass the other party's desk, just so they don't accidentally run into them. They might ask the boss to reassign them to avoid having to interact with that other person. There are many variations on this theme that people typically employ when in conflict. The challenge is that they might be hard to spot, precisely because the avoidance behaviours keep them out of sight and out of mind.

Some relational warning signs can, however, be easier to detect because they're much more obvious. Let's take the example of a production meeting in which a production manager (or location manager, head of costumes, second AD, etc.) has been ignoring their own emotional and physical warning signs too long, due to an earlier conflict with another key team member. They are deliberately unresponsive towards the person with whom they are having difficulty. Let's call one Frank and the other Tom. Frank may give Tom the silent treatment, be deliberately unresponsive to direct questions, or Frank may start making Tom the target of snarky comments whenever Tom offers input. He may openly disagree, challenge, or argue with Tom. When Tom speaks, Frank may roll his eyes, cross his arms defensively, or deliberately begin shuffling pieces of paper. Frank may demonstrate disrespect by indulging in distractions or otherwise showing he isn't listening or taking Tom seriously. Or he may start engaging in trash-talking Tom behind his back. You can imagine how these behaviours might be received and how they could impact the relationship between the two, or indeed between any others present at the production meetings. One person's issue soon can become the whole production's.

Through your own prior experience, you may already be familiar with the wide range of actions or reactions that signal possible danger in a relationship. The key point here is that the behaviours eventually impact not only the person who has been ignoring their own internal/emotional warning signs, but also the others in the group, team, or company. More people are indirectly drawn into the conflict when the behaviour starts affecting them, too. Innocent bystanders start resenting the toxic environment. The stakes are raised, and soon the whole workplace becomes entangled if things don't get resolved.

What the Four Warning Signs Mean

These, in a nutshell, are the four successive levels of warning signs that conflict is taking place: emotional, physical, behavioural, and relational. In conflict, people seldom stop to take stock of a situation, retracing their steps to figure out how they got to the point where they're no longer willing to even talk to one another. But your awareness of these early warning signs can alert you to the fact that something may be happening right now that's worth investigating. If something's wrong, your mind and body are probably telling you to do something about it. The warning signs tell you it's time to exercise self-care, and the longer you postpone taking action, the more intense and unavoidable the signals will become.

As mentioned previously, many people are uncomfortable talking openly about their feelings. Some families or entire cultures are so ill at ease about feelings, they seldom, if ever, discuss them. Some are only comfortable talking about their feelings with therapists or other professionals, because they feel particularly vulnerable. In any case, feelings (your own and others') should be acknowledged, even honoured, because they play a vital role in caretaking and preventive maintenance in any relationship. Respect your feelings and their noble purpose. Negative feelings towards a person or situation are just a sign that something needs to be fixed. Like any bodily aches or pain, if you ignore your feelings, hoping they'll go away, the symptoms will get progressively worse over time. Heed the conflict warning signs promptly because the consequences can be severe later on.

Should I Get Help, and When?

Conflict is never fun and is seldom easy, so often the first instinct is to seek help. Sometimes help is recommended, but it's not always necessary if you have the core skills. This book is meant to equip you with the fundamental knowledge and tools to prevent most disagreements from escalating, and to navigate your way through any existing conflicts. Part of dealing with conflict successfully, though, is an ability to discern when it's appropriate to try resolving a conflict on your own, and when you should seek assistance. We will learn how to assess a conflict in this section, but first we need to dispel a couple of widely held myths. More specifically, we need to challenge some misperceptions about getting help with conflict resolution.

Four Myths of Conflict

There are four main reasons why people avoid seeking help with conflict, and they spring from a commonly held mythology. It's worth debunking the stories if it encourages people to get help to deal with their interpersonal issues.

Myth #1: If I can't deal with this conflict on my own, that must mean there's something wrong with me. This notion is entirely unfounded because conflict prevention and resolution skills are just that: skills. All proficiencies, whether it's directing, memorizing lines, or non-linear editing, are learned over time. If you didn't master conflict resolution the very first time (or few times) you tried, congratulations! You're normal. There is nothing wrong with you.

People are not born with conflict resolution skills. They have to acquire them. Sure, some seem to have an innate ability to grasp the concepts more readily than others, but they still require effort to discover, learn, practice, and improve. So, if you don't think you are good at resolving conflict, it's not because Myth #1 is true; it is simply because most of us never get the training to develop these competencies. (This may be changing, albeit slowly, with some progressive school boards incorporating basic conflict resolution techniques as early as elementary school.)

Unfortunately, most of us first learned a form of conflict resolution in a family environment. This might be fine, depending of course on how conflict was handled at home. For those of us raised up until the 2000s, however, it's likely that sibling or parental conflict was met with denial, punishment, authoritarian rules, yelling, fighting, or some combination of these. Only a small minority of adults spent the time, effort, and/or money to ensure their children knew how to successfully work through conflict by the time they left home. (Don't blame your parents; that's probably how they were raised, too.) It's more than likely you were taught instead to defend yourself, to stand up to others. For most people, school experience with conflict can be summed up in a few words: Detentions. Suspensions. Bullying. Peer pressure.

You've probably never heard of a high school dialogue club, but most of us have encountered a high school debating club. That's because of our society: we value debating, which is essentially the skill of winning arguments. Dialogue, on the other hand, is essentially the skill of achieving mutual understanding, which is a very different thing. The former may be useful in the short term, but the latter is a far more desirable and helpful long-term solution. (For an eye-opening and eminently readable discourse on the state of things, read Deborah Tannen's *The Argument Culture*. For any documentarians reading this, we suggest it would make a fascinating subject.)

By the time you reach adulthood, you have had very little (if any) education or experience in preventing or resolving conflict in the most effective way. No wonder it's hard! Sending people out into the world without any training in conflict prevention or resolution, then expecting them to figure it out as they go, is a bit like giving the latest-generation 8k digital camera to a kid who has never learned the basics of cinematography and expecting her to shoot *Lawrence of Arabia*.

Myth #1, then, clearly isn't true. If you can't deal with this conflict on your own because you don't have the skills to do so, you aren't bad or wrong, and you don't need to be fixed, because you aren't broken. On the contrary, it means you are reassuringly just like the rest of us.

Myth #2: If I need to get help with this conflict, that means I am weak. Again, this is emphatically not the case. If you need to get help with a conflict, then it just means you have realistically assessed the situation and determined that it might be a bad idea to tackle it alone. If your intuition and intellect are telling you that you won't be able to successfully work through this conflict without getting some kind of support or assistance, then you have made a good judgment call. You are not weak. On the contrary, you are rational, discerning, and strong enough to admit your doubts around the conflict. The key is to follow up and actively seek help. (Where to go for help is covered later in Part One.)

Myth #3: If I need to get help with this conflict, then I'll be perceived as weak by the other person(s). Busted again! Reaching out for support in any difficult situation is an intelligent and self-loving thing to do. If someone is suggesting (or telling you) that you are somehow weak for seeking help in dealing with a conflict, try to have compassion for that person too. If human behaviour is the outward reflection of what's inside, then the individual who puts another down for getting help is probably making the same judgment about themselves, i.e., "I would think I must be weak if I needed outside help." (See Myth #2!) Recognize that they're probably experiencing some internal distress, do what you need to do to get the conflict resolved, and ignore the name-calling.

It's possible that no one is actually thinking or saying that you are weak for seeking assistance. Maybe it's just your fear of their judgment talking. Be open to the possibility that they may be thinking differently. They might well consider your mature handling of the situation as quite admirable (even if they might be unwilling to admit it at the time). They might be grateful for taking the steps necessary to save the relationship. They might be wishing they'd thought of it first.

Myth #4: We don't need to make such a big deal out of this — we can just talk and work things out. This may indeed be true; as long as the matter truly isn't a major, recurring issue, you can probably sit down together and work it out. The key here is not to be too quick to dismiss it as "no big deal." Disputes that haven't already spiraled out of control can be handled on your own if you remember to keep focused on the issue, otherwise there is always a risk that the disagreement may escalate into a conflict, and so on. These key skills are the focus of Part Three.

So can you tell whether or not it really is a big deal for yourself or the other person? And what if it is a big deal? Are confidence and good intentions enough to get you through? Worse still, what if you're just telling yourself it's not a big deal, in order to cover up your concerns and to mask your fear of not knowing what to do about the situation?

Again, we'll delve into assessing and evaluating conflicts soon enough. If it really isn't such a big deal, go ahead and grab a beer or a coffee. Have the necessary, and maybe difficult, conversation. Use the skills outlined in this book, and you'll resolve it successfully. If for any reason you don't nail it immediately, keep trying. Practice! It's unlikely you'll make things any worse as long as you stick with what you'll learn. You can always get help afterwards if you need it.

If the matter is truly serious or important in any way, the worst thing you can do is ignore it. Get the help. (The next section outlines the different types of help available, and there's lots out there for any budget.) If you're not confident about being able to manage it on your own, plenty of assistance is yours for the asking.

What Kind of Help to Get: Conflict Resolution Processes

The good news is that there are many equally effective processes, models, and approaches in the world of conflict resolution. The bad news is that knowing where to start can feel overwhelming. To keep it simple, we've distilled it down to the following essential list of options, how they differ, and how they work:

Problem solving, or negotiation: With this process, which is essentially a joint decision-making exercise, you and the person(s) with whom you are having the issue sit down together and work things out on your own. There is no third-party involvement. You use your skills to understand each other's perspectives and figure out what is not working between you and how to resolve it. You can use everything in this book to help you resolve this conflict on your own through negotiation. Review the skills and the basic conflict resolution process presented in Part Three, and go for it.

Despite the clichéd notion of negotiation as two opponents battling it out on opposite sides of a table, it's really a collaborative problem-solving process, as the name implies. The goal is to achieve an objectively fair, win-win solution out of a range of viable options that you develop together, thus repairing and strengthening the relationship now and for the future.

We've presented negotiation as a sort of antidote to conflict, one of several proven alternative dispute resolution (ADR) processes. But it can also be an invaluable preventive measure, and we heartily recommend negotiating the terms of any creative collaboration up-front, long before any problems arise. By negotiate the terms of the relationship we don't just mean the financial, legal, or technical aspects (although those are clearly important to figure out beforehand, too). We suggest that negotiating the practical, day-to-day functioning of the partnership can be critical to the short- and long-term health of the collaboration. In addition to agreeing on how you might share screen credit, for example, you might also want to establish norms for handling conflicts. (What do we do if or when things get heated? Is swearing acceptable, as long as it's not directed at anyone in particular, or is it out of bounds under any circumstances? Should we take time-outs, or keep working through it? How early should we bring in a neutral third party to help settle any disagreement?) You might also want to define your respective roles, divide up responsibilities, or clarify your expectations. The sky's the limit as far as what you could negotiate – just as long as you do it.

We stress this because it's our experience that relatively few creative partnerships begin with such a mutual understanding. This is unfortunate, because it's well worth the modest time and effort that discussing any such agreement might take. Many (perhaps most) fail to negotiate their collaborations ahead of time, usually out of some sort of fear or anxiety. They may not want to risk upsetting the other party, they may be afraid of negotiating poorly, or they may worry about looking presumptuous or mistrustful. It's also common for people to enter into a working relationship with a number of untested assumptions about how things will work, which later becomes a source of conflict. There are many reasons why people hesitate to negotiate, and while they're all perfectly understandable, they're also generally unfounded.

Conflict management coaching. Let's say your assessment of the conflict indicates that you can probably resolve the issue on your own, but you think you might need to sharpen some of your dialogue and negotiation skills or prepare for challenging and unexpected scenarios. Perhaps you just want to get independent advice about the conflict from someone before you try resolving it without a third party present. In these cases, conflict coaching is an excellent option. Here, a conflict resolution practitioner works with you behind the scenes, mentoring you in the desired skill areas. Together you can better prepare to approach the other person to work through your issues in a collaborative, productive, and positive manner. All parties in a conflict are welcome to use their own conflict coach(es). You may want to try conflict coaching if you're afraid of letting your emotions get the better of you and saying something to the other person that might trigger them. Maybe a coworker has been consistently late, and previous attempts at changing the behaviour have been unsuccessful. A conflict coach might also remind you of the steps to resolving a negotiation fairly; work with you to develop multiple options for a win-win outcome; or otherwise guide you in keeping the negotiation friendly, mutually supportive, and low on the emotional VU meter.

Facilitation. With facilitation, a neutral third party is directly involved in the negotiation. This is unlike conflict coaching, where the third party is only indirectly involved and, in working closely with one party, is somewhat aligned. The facilitation option is particularly helpful when your assessment of the conflict indicates that there is a trouble spot(s) around one or more of the levels of emotion, trust, the conflict history, or its power dynamic. Perhaps you anticipate it will be difficult to get through a conversation and resolve the issue without the aid of an outside party. A facilitator is impartial and non-biased, and they will assist the two of you in staying on track and keeping the conversation focused, meaningful, and productive. In other words, a facilitator helps both parties equally with their communication, so that you can get more directly to what needs to be fixed, and fix it.

One appropriate use of this approach might be a negotiation over a writing or producing partnership, for example. This is one area, in our experience, where prospective partners commonly disagree; it's also where the level of emotion is ramped up a notch or two due to creative pride and, of course, the income potential at stake. (Money is one area where people can get very emotional indeed.) In such cases, the history of conflict may be virtually nonexistent, and the power dynamic may be perfectly equal between the prospective partners, but tension still surfaces. The facilitator's role here may be to help the parties agree on what constitutes a fair split of writing credit or net profits from the picture — because what might seem fair to one partner may not seem fair to another. In such situations, the facilitator might work with the parties to find some mutually agreed upon standard of fairness or to implement a way to assess and evaluate the proportions of work involved.

Note that the facilitator is exclusively interested in the process of the negotiation and has no attachment to the content or outcome of the negotiation. The facilitator is not aligned with either party. The would-be partners are still doing the "heavy lifting" in terms of the actual problem-solving and decision-making, and the facilitator is simply there to ensure that the way they make decisions is effective. The facilitator might help the partners determine a method for deciding the issues to be discussed, but has no input on the issues themselves.

Mediation: Sometimes an assessment of a conflict will indicate that some or even all of the dimensions of emotions, trust, history, and power are challenging. In such cases you know right away that you'll need help with more than just the communication aspect. You will need a third party to help you navigate through powerful emotional currents, rebuild trust, identify the patterns and dynamics that contributed to the history of the conflict, and address any power imbalances that exist between the parties. In short, mediation goes way beyond communication issues. A mediator will impartially assist both or all parties equally in dealing with all four factors. Like a facilitator, a mediator is unbiased. As with facilitation, the mediator will expect the parties to do the work to resolve the conflict on their own, but will take on a more active role in guiding them through the process.

Because the emotional (and sometimes legal) stakes are always higher when mediation is the appropriate option, most mediations begin and end with some paperwork: a confidentiality agreement typically starts the process, and a formal agreement on how issues were resolved between the parties ends the process. This, however, is almost always a better route than litigation, because the adversarial nature of court actions can increase mutual antagonism and cause irreparable damage to personal relationships. Patching things up after long weeks, months, or even years of conflict can be difficult if not impossible.

Group intervention: Sometimes a conflict situation involves more than just interpersonal issues between two or a few people; sometimes it's the whole cast, crew, production company, or studio. In these instances, a group intervention is the appropriate option. It may or may not include individuals using any of the previously described options, but it will certainly address the whole group. Many teams and organizations can benefit from some form of group intervention, not necessarily specifically for handling conflict; preventive group interventions can also be held for team-building, decision-making, improving accountability, assessing team role interactions, and so forth. A group intervention to specifically address conflict can be a complex process, but at a basic level the following is what you can expect with a group intervention: The entire team contributes to an assessment of the conflict/current situation; an intervention is designed based on the results and interpretation of this assessment; the success of the intervention is assessed and modified where necessary; and a follow-up plan is implemented to ensure that the team remains healthy.

Negotiation or problem-solving, conflict coaching, facilitation, mediation, and group intervention are all proven methods of working through conflict, in order to emerge as a stronger and more productive creative collaboration than ever. One of the many benefits of these processes is that the responsibility and control of the outcome is always in the hands of the people in conflict. No one tells them what to do, dictates an outcome, or makes decisions for them. In other words, you get to figure out what is wrong and fix it! Through these approaches, people can actually get closer, relationships become stronger, trust increases, and ultimately, more great entertainment is made.

Assessing a Conflict Situation

The relevant questions, then, are these: How do you figure out whether or not you need to get help in dealing with a particular conflict situation? And which of these conflict resolution and management approaches is most appropriate for it? It would help to have a tool to help you to realistically assess the situation as objectively as any subjective participant can, under the present circumstances. In the Appendix you'll find a *Conflict Assessment Worksheet* specifically for this purpose. It considers four key dimensions of the conflict: emotions, trust, history, and power.

Let's examine each of these factors in turn, beginning with the level or intensity of the *emotions* involved. The first and easiest to determine is your own emotional level. Are you still feeling fairly calm about the situation? Mildly annoyed, but not enraged? Disappointed, but not full of anger and blame? If your emotional VU meter indicates that things are not going well but are not yet off the chart, that's one thing. If your feelings meter is consistently peaking in the red zone, that's quite another. Next, to the best of your ability, consider the emotional level of the other person(s) involved in the conflict. Overall, what is your assessment? On a five-point scale, are the emotions relatively low (1), or extremely high (5)?

Next, consider the *level of trust* between the parties to the conflict. Do you still feel a healthy level of trust in them, and vice versa? Do you have the sense that they still genuinely want the best for you, even if the two of you are in disagreement? Do you believe that they will work for the ultimate good of the unit, show, or company? Or are you thinking that they are no longer trustworthy, their own agenda has become their prime concern, and they don't really care how you are doing in the midst of the conflict? If you score 1 for both parties, then the trust is relatively unbroken and healthy. Anywhere upwards of 3 may be cause for concern, even if only one of the parties feels that way. Mistrust is mistrust, whether or not it runs in both directions.

Third, look at the *history* of your conflict. Is it negligible, or extensive? Is this conflict a relatively recent one, in which bad feelings haven't really had the chance to develop? Is it a recurring issue? Are other people not yet involved? If they are, have they taken sides? Do you still feel reasonably confident you'll be able to resolve these issues with the right skills and approach? Or, is there a long, ugly trajectory to this conflict, with lots of negativity and resentment built up over time, with cast and crew members, friends, and others getting involved and contributing to the problem? Again, a low score indicates little to no prior history, whereas a higher score indicates a substantial history to be taken well into account.

Finally, take a look at the *dynamic of power* in your relationship. Do you feel that the power distribution is more or less equal and balanced? If so, you'll probably give this dimension a low score, perhaps 1 or 2. Do they have some sort of authority over you in terms of their influence or decision-making ability, or vice versa? Do they have some coercive force at their disposal, such as information that you'd prefer remain private? Then your score would probably be on the higher end of the five-point scale. Consider, for example, your role in the production; are you a PA or First AD? Showrunner or junior writer? Executive Producer or Line Producer? Do you have any concerns about expressing yourself honestly or fears about asking for what you want? Do you find that you muzzle yourself and avoid speaking up, worried that it will make things worse for you because of the other person's power, role, status, or authority? If the conflict is with your producer, then they may have a significant power advantage. If it's with one of the other Heads of Department, there may be little or no imbalance of power. Depending on your answers to these and other key questions, something about the relationship may contribute to a power imbalance in any given situation.

The trick when trying to decide whether you will need some help in dealing with this conflict (and what kind) is to figure out where you are with respect to the emotions, trust, history, and power. The *Conflict Assessment Worksheet* allows you to evaluate your situation by literally adding it all up. Each of the four criteria are measured on a five-point, Likert-type scale. A total score of 4 out of 20 possible points clearly means all of these dimensions of the conflict are in good shape, so it's reasonably safe to assume you can respond by either trying to manage it yourselves, or by seeking conflict management coaching or some equally unobtrusive assistance.

If one or more of these key dimensions are on sufficiently shaky ground, you'll respond differently, probably by seeking more active, professional help. It is your assessment that will help you determine what kind of help or support you should seek. Lower scores on most factors but a maximum (i.e., 5) score in one particular area may merit at least some form of outside assistance, like facilitation. A score closer to 20 out of 20 possible points means you probably shouldn't even attempt to resolve the issue(s) on your own without at least consulting some experienced, professional help before you begin, and, more likely, engaging help to guide both or all of the parties at every step of the way.

In addition to the Conflict Assessment Worksheet, we have prepared a *Conflict Assistance Chart* (Table 1, below) to help you determine what kind of assisted conflict resolution process is most appropriate to your specific situation. You can download additional copies of these and other free resources at the Fifth House Group website, by visiting http://www.fifthhousegroup.com/resources).

Factor	Coaching	Negotiation	Facilitation	Mediation
Emotions	Any	Low to Medium	Medium	High
Trust Levels	Any	Good to Medium	Medium	Low
History	Any	None or Positive	Some	Some or Negative
Power Imbalance	Any	None or Some	Some	Yes

Table 1: Conflict Assistance Chart.

To better understand how conflict situations can be assessed, let's look at a few examples:

1. INT. WRITERS' ROOM - DAY.

ALEX and CASEY are part of a small team of writers on a popular sitcom. Both have a background in stand-up comedy and were hired at about the same time. The writers' room has an informal, mostly relaxed atmosphere, with jokes flying thick and fast even when the writers aren't focused on the script. Occasionally loud and boisterous, especially as the shooting deadline nears, there is a palpable competitiveness to some of the conversations. After a few weeks and episodes, Alex feels Casey is increasingly dismissive and harshly critical, putting down Alex's contribution at every opportunity. This is more obvious when Jessie, the Head Writer, is present, and Alex perceives it's because Casey wants to impress Jessie and solidify their relationship.

If Alex were to evaluate the conflict using the scoring system and worksheet provided, the result might be the following:

Factor	Coaching	Negotiation	Facilitation	Mediation
Emotions	Any	Low to Medium	Medium	High

Trust Levels	Any	Good to Medium	Medium	Low
History	Any	None or Positive	Some	Some or Negative
Power Imbalance	Any	None or Some	Some	Yes

Table 2: Scene 1 conflict assessment.

In this scenario, Alex could choose to address the conflict alone through negotiation, without any third-party intervention. This would work well if Alex prepares ahead of time, perhaps reads a few relevant articles, and consults some preparation materials to stay on track throughout the process. Alternatively, Alex could choose to seek some conflict management coaching.

2. EXT. STUDIO PARKING LOT - NIGHT.

The end of another long, hard day on set; cast and crew are exhausted and testy. KELLY, the show's producer, has a close eye on the clock as the MOW has run overtime for two consecutive days and is starting to go seriously over budget. Kelly has already had more than one conversation with Director PAT about this, and Pat has stood firmly over a desire for emotional authenticity and to push the actors to their best performances while still "in the zone."

Each has a begrudging respect for the other's work, having bumped heads on previous shows. Both would prefer to work with others but Kelly did not hire Pat, who was the studio's choice. Kelly worries that Pat may go crying to the studio, undermining Kelly's authority and job security. Pat fears that Kelly's obsession with the bottom line will be reflected in the show's quality and, ultimately, Pat's "mad genius" reputation. Pat is also concerned about being replaced; it's Pat's first big gig after emerging from rehab and lengthy underemployment.

An assessment of the conflict between the producer and director might be summarized thus:

Factor	Coaching	Negotiation	Facilitation	Mediation
Emotions	Any	Low to Medium	Medium	High

Factor	Coaching	Negotiation	Facilitation	Mediation
Trust Levels	Any	Good to Medium	Medium	Low
History	Any	None or Positive	Some	Some or Negative
Power Imbalance	Any	None or Some	Some	Yes

Table 3: Scene 2 conflict assessment.

In this scenario, Kelly or Pat should choose to address the conflict with some third-party assistance, likely facilitation. This would work well if they prepared themselves ahead of time with the facilitator, so they both go into the facilitation with the clear goals of listening to understand each other and communicating in order to resolve the issues before them.

3. INT. PRODUCTION OFFICE - DAY.

JEANNE is Production Manager on a high-profile, big-budget feature. She is in a quandary about RICHARD, an old-school cinematographer who is the equally high profile Director's right-hand man. Richard and the Director are close friends and came as a matched set; Richard knows that if anything should upset him, the Director may walk out in support. Richard has long made a habit of lewd or sexist remarks aimed at female cast and crew members, and either the director does not hear or chooses to ignore them.

Jeanne herself was the victim of unwelcome comments and expletives after taking Richard aside immediately following early reports of the unwanted behaviour. She needs to address the issue urgently, but this is one of Jeanne's first PM roles for a major studio, and she wants to gain their confidence and secure continued work. She would prefer to resolve the situation on her own, without dragging the absentee producer or studio executives into the fray. Much is at stake here, for her, the studio, and the rest of the cast and crew.

If Jeanne were to evaluate the conflict using the scoring system and worksheet provided, the result may look something like the following:

Factor	Coaching	Negotiation	Facilitation	Mediation
Emotions	Any	Low to Medium	Medium	High

Factor	Coaching	Negotiation	Facilitation	Mediation
Trust Levels	Any	Good to Medium	Medium	Low
History	Any	None or Positive	Some	Some or Negative
Power Imbalance	Any	None or Some	Some	Yes

Table 4: Scene 3 conflict assessment.

In this scenario, Jeanne would be wise to address the conflict with some third-party intervention, likely mediation. Because there are clear personality differences between her and Richard, a history of conflict, and strong feelings of fear on her part, the issues between them involve more than just communication. There are definite interpersonal and psychological aspects to this conflict.

Where Can I Get the Help I Need?

One place to go for immediate assistance is our website, www.fifthhousegroup.com, where we have posted numerous how-to articles and other free resources for creatives and those who live or work with them. Among these tools are additional blank copies of the worksheets used in this book.

Another option is simply to search the web, using terms such as "conflict resolution services," "alternative dispute resolution services," "community mediation services," "volunteer mediators [your city here]," etc., and follow those leads. You can search for services in your region specifically, or let Google and other search engines such as Bing provide geographically relevant sponsored links (advertisements) and regular, non-sponsored results through geolocation.

A third option is to check out your local college or university. Many institutions now offer courses, certificates, and degrees in the field of conflict resolution, and in addition to their academic programs some also offer free, low-cost, or geared-to-income conflict resolution services so graduating students can gain practical experience in the field.

Whichever route you choose, there are many resources out there to support you in resolving a conflict. If you can pay full fare, you will never have a problem finding a professional conflict resolution practitioner; the investment will pay dividends in both the short and longer term. If you don't have that kind of money, with just a bit of effort, you will be able to find free, low-cost or geared-to-income assistance through the many community-based mediation programs that exist in many parts of the world.

Back to Ones: Summary

Wherever there are two or more people working together, there is room for conflict, especially in film and TV, which are necessarily collaborative efforts. Conflict and its side effects have affected some of the most successful creative teams and individuals, productions, and entire studios or networks. Conflict has also played a significant role in effectively ending some careers prematurely. The costs of conflict can be enormous, not merely at a financial level (which can be staggering in extreme cases), but extending beyond the people directly involved to encompass audiences and the broader community. The ripple effects can be long-lasting and profound.

Conflict isn't mere disagreement; it's a signal that something needs to change, either in a particular situation or within a relationship (or maybe both). In fact, the right amount of productive conflict may be essential to successful creative partnerships. Research shows that there may be reluctance for creative team members to commit to a course of action or decision if ideas under discussion have not been well and truly put to the test through dialogue, debate, and even passionate argument.

The key is to ensure relationships and conflicts remain healthy. To avoid having them take a destructive turn, it's essential to differentiate between disagreement, conflict, and harassment or bullying. Understanding how conflicts can escalate – often unintentionally – gives us the tools to prevent them from doing so. It allows us to keep them from spiraling out of control when they do occur, and to manage them effectively from the beginning.

To be effective at conflict resolution, it's also important to recognize four types of warning signs, which begin with our own inner emotional state, i.e., our feelings. If emotions around a person or situation aren't addressed adequately, the warning signals will radiate progressively outward, first becoming physical manifestations, then informing our behaviours, and ultimately impacting our relationships. At each successive level these cues alert us to the fact that something is wrong, and the sooner we can recognize them, the quicker and easier we can reduce or eliminate the symptoms and manage and resolve the conflict.

You can attempt to resolve the situation directly with the other person(s) through negotiation or problem-solving. If you don't feel confident in your conflict resolution skills or your ability to manage the situation on your own, help is readily available. There are many sources of support available to you, ranging from free or inexpensive resources like books and websites (including the Fifth House Group website), to paid professional assistance from conflict resolution practitioners in your local area.

It's useful to be able to determine when it's appropriate to enlist outside help managing or resolving a conflict, and the best approach or method for your particular situation. You can objectively assess and evaluate a conflict situation using four key criteria: the level of emotional intensity in the conflict; the levels of trust and the power dynamic between the parties involved; and the history of the conflict. This information will also help you determine which of several modes of conflict resolution assistance may be most appropriate to you, including (but not limited to) negotiation, conflict coaching, mediation, facilitation, and alternative dispute resolution (ADR) mechanisms.

PART TWO:
THE INNER MECHANICS OF CONFLICT

Learning outcomes: By the end of this section, you should have the skills, knowledge, and attitudes necessary to

- analyze the role of emotions in conflict situations and interpret a range of feelings relating to conflict;
- explain the role of needs in conflict and discover the needs of parties to a conflict;
- define and interpret strategies used in conflict situations; and
- distinguish authentic feelings from blaming feelings.

Decoding Conflict: Feelings, Needs, and Strategies

What really happens inside of people who are in conflict? This may seem like an odd or obvious question, but it's an important one. When in conflict, it's hard to keep track of what is happening internally; thoughts, feelings, and speech happen at lightning speed, reactions get triggered left and right, and soon the parties end up not talking about what they really need to talk about.

People can suddenly feel provoked or attacked and experience an urge to fight back. They might not even be aware of the real, underlying issue that they really need to talk about, only that something is wrong and they feel upset or vaguely uncomfortable. In conflict, all kinds of strong feelings can easily overwhelm us, leading participants to say or do things they might later regret. Even if they don't necessarily feel remorse for their words or actions, they will likely realize that they didn't help the situation. In retrospect, such impulsive reactions might only make matters worse. This section is about understanding what is actually taking place on a personal — indeed, intimate — level when people are in conflict.

There are three essential components involved in any conflict: feelings, needs, and strategies. Each has a specific role and purpose in the context of conflict.

Feelings, as discussed earlier, indicate that something is not quite right with a given situation. More precisely, they alert us when we have needs that are being unmet or are threatened in some way. Then, when we experience unmet needs, we apply strategies to meet or restore those needs. It's deceptively straightforward, because all conflict really does boil down to are these three basic components. The simplicity of their interaction is misleading because most people are unaware of what these three mechanisms are, what they actually signify, or how they work, making every conflict feel so much more confusing, chaotic, and complex.

As with conflict resolution skills, we are seldom given the opportunity to learn about the true genius of our feelings, never mind needs and strategies, as we move through our lives. So it's not surprising that we continue acting on them reflexively, behaving impulsively instead of thoughtfully, rarely pausing to decode each element and using its hidden meaning to our mutual benefit. But if we are able to pause long enough to recognize the signals and interpret the feelings, needs, and strategies, then we can access a vast amount of valuable information about ourselves and the other people in our lives. A brief analysis will deconstruct how it all works.

The Role of Feelings

Like conflict itself, feelings aren't capricious; they don't just randomly appear. We may not always appreciate or fully understand them, but they have underlying causes. As discussed earlier, feelings serve as one indicator of the extent to which a particular situation is acceptable or healthy. These feelings can range from calm or contentment, to low-intensity discomfort, all the way to rage, complete with a concomitant array of physical symptoms. As quick as we are sometimes to dismiss our human emotions, they've actually been critical to the development and survival of our species. Feelings are part of an ancient, ingenious, and virtually fail-safe self-protection mechanism. Their very specific function is to monitor our well-being on a moment-by-moment basis, interpreting the sensory input and responding accordingly if there is potential harm. Fear, for example, is arguably the most powerful. It will cause you to back away from a wild animal or avoid excessive heights, keeping you safe from those and a host of other potential dangers.

In general, and with specific regard to conflict, emotions protect us by alerting us to whether the person(s) we are with, or the situation we are in, is healthy or unhealthy, safe or dangerous. To be more accurate, your feelings indicate whether or not your needs are currently being met at any given point in time. Fear, for example, lets you know that your need for safety and security is not being met, or is somehow being threatened. To invoke our previous analogy, your feelings are the VU meter that indicates how you are doing with regard to a person(s) or situation. As long as the indicator is relatively inactive and in the low end, your needs are probably being met. When the meter starts to fluctuate wildly or peaks into the red zone, your needs are not being met.

To test this theory, let's do a quick experiment. Take a moment to think about someone, or a situation, that normally feels good for you. What specific feelings do you experience? See if any of the feelings in the word cloud in Figure 5 resonate with you in regard to the person/situation you currently have in mind:

involved
engrossed
friendly
tender
warm
intrigued
interested
entranced
optimistic
expectant
alert
absorbed
AFFECTIONATE
open-hearted
encouraged
loving
ENGAGED
compassionate
enchanted
sympathetic
spellbound
curious
HOPEFUL
stimulated
fascinated

Figure 5: Positive feelings.

Adapted from Center for Nonviolent Communication, Website: www.cnvc.org, Email: cnvc@cnvc.org, Phone: +1.505.244.4041

If you identified any or all of these feelings with the person or the situation you thought about for this exercise, then those emotions are telling you that the person(s) or situation is probably healthy for you. The result of an interaction would be generally positive, and there is little or no threat of physical or psychological/emotional harm. It means that most of your needs are being met – needs like respect, love, acceptance, friendship, and so on, all the way down the list. (The variety of needs, and their role, is examined in the next section.)

Now we're going to change the experiment and have you think about a person(s) or situation about which you have very different feelings — the negative kind. Again, see if any words from the word cloud in Figure 6 are applicable to what you are experiencing:

Figure 6: Negative feelings.

Adapted from Center for Nonviolent Communication, Website: www.cnvc.org, Email: cnvc@cnvc.org, Phone: +1.505.244.4041

If you are having these sorts of feelings, especially if you are experiencing them continuously or chronically, then that person(s) or situation probably isn't healthy for you. These emotions are meant to keep you safe from physical or psychological (emotional) harm. They mean that one or more need is not being met – you are probably not having your need for respect, love, acceptance, friendship, etc., satisfied.

When you think of the full spectrum of feelings that humans experience in terms of an early warning system, you can see how important it is for giving us some very accurate and useful information. The emotions themselves can be a reliable indicator, especially if you know what the discomfort signifies, but when you take into account their relative intensity, the safety/security information received is that much clearer and more powerful. Just as a driver would be foolish to ignore a car's plunging gas gauge or fast-rising engine thermometer, this information should be taken seriously in order to avoid even more unpleasant consequences. Heeding the vehicle's instrument panel – or your emotional VU meter – is a crucial early step in taking good care of ourselves and, ultimately, each other.

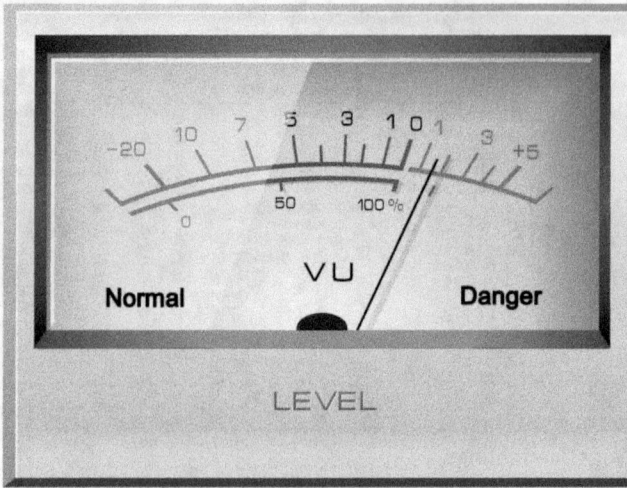

Figure 7: The feelings VU meter (analog version).

As the discomfort and intensity levels rise, the urgency of paying attention increases commensurately.

The Role of Needs

We have now seen how our feelings serve as a safety mechanism that lets us know whether the particular people or situations are either good or bad for us. But what does "good for us" mean, more specifically? What does it mean when we decide, "It's good for me to be around this person," or, "It's a good situation for me to be in"?

On closer analysis, what these expressions fundamentally mean is that in the moment our needs are being met. This raises a subsequent question: what type of needs are being met? And what are "needs," anyway?

To answer the last question first, needs are states of being that are essential for (psychological) health, safety, and well-being.

We'll come back to the first question in a moment, but first it's important to make a distinction between needs and wants. These terms are sometimes used interchangeably. Remember, a need is necessary for our psychological health: if a particular need isn't met, you will experience genuine emotional pain, and in extremely unhealthy situations you might even feel physically uncomfortable. A want is more like a desire — it would be pleasant to have, and sometimes it even seems crucial — but you could, if you had to, live without it. As we shall see in the next section, "wants" are really code for "strategies," but we'll get to that in due course.

In the meantime, know that needs are "non-negotiables" for human beings. Like air, food, water, or shelter, if you take them away, we suffer. Deprived of these, our physical and mental health and well-being are at serious risk. But our complex human needs can extend beyond those basic bodily requirements and into more abstract territory. Consider Figure 8's sampling of human feeling-needs:

Figure 8: Feeling-needs.

Adapted from the Center for Nonviolent Communication. Website: www.cnvc.org, Email: cnvc@cnvc.org, Phone: +1.505-244-4041

Some might argue that these are wants: nice to have, but not necessary for our mental health and well-being. But feeling-needs are very real, and they're equally applicable to all of humanity, regardless of race, culture, ethnicity, religion, etc. If you're not convinced, imagine yourself stranded on a deserted island. Can you picture what might happen to you psychologically and emotionally if you had to live for a prolonged period of time without any other human contact or connection? Eventually you might have some sort of breakdown. Or consider acceptance: if you've ever experienced being ostracized in your life—perhaps you were the new kid who didn't fit in at school, or you were otherwise set apart from the "in" crowd—you know how painful it can be to live without acceptance. In extreme cases, being cast out of a social group or tribe could result in serious physical harm, either from violence, or the elements, or wild animals. Some might argue that you could live forever without appreciation, but, truthfully, if you have ever worked long and hard for something without getting at least a token of recognition for it, then you know how important appreciation really is. Without it, you feel emotional pain, and you probably suffer in a way that feels just as real as any hunger, injury, or other physical sensation.

From this perspective, you can see why we call these needs the non-negotiables for human beings everywhere. We just don't always share the same set of priorities. Some of these needs will be more or less important to you than others, and someone else will rank them differently. For one actor, the predominant driving force may be the need to turn in an emotionally resonant performance, while for another the most important consideration may be camaraderie, and for still another the main need might be public recognition.

Imagine a life where some or all of our base-level physiological needs were not met—what a misery! Fortunately, those of us in the developed nations have most (if not all) of our more basic housing, nutrition, and security needs met, so we can afford the relative luxury of spending mental and physical energy seeking to satisfy our higher-order social, personal, and/or self-realization needs. Each of us is unique in our own specific priorities, but we are all alike in that these emotional health and wellness needs are equally critical to our personal sense of well-being. What would it be like if you had to endure life without ever meeting some or all of the needs associated with Connection in Figure 8?

Now think about the people and situations in your daily life and, more specifically, in your industry. If you think about them from this perspective, you will more than likely recognize that the people and situations that push your emotional VU meter into the red zone are those that don't allow your needs to be met. Here are just a few examples:

- If you feel negatively about a cast member showing up late, it may be because you feel your own time isn't valued, since you and others show up on time and wait around even though the rest of you have other things to do and places you could be. You have a need for respect, and it isn't being met.

- If you are frustrated over your creative input being disregarded, it may be because you feel you aren't being heard or acknowledged for your contributions. You have a need for acknowledgement or validation that isn't being met.

- If you are feeling anxious or uncomfortable when important decisions are being made without you (or you're being consistently out-voted), it may be because you feel like you are apart from the team, or perhaps you feel powerless. Depending on which of these is truer for you, you may have a need to feel membership (a sense of belonging) or agency – or both – that isn't being satisfied in these situations.

The key here is to first try to pinpoint exactly what the feeling is, and then identify the underlying need that is causing it. Yes, the situation or person may be contributing to the feeling somehow, but they're not directly causing it. The challenge is to remember that no matter how frustrated (or angry, lonely, etc.) you might feel, *the other person is never the actual problem.* It's their outward behaviour – in other words, what they're saying or doing – that is the source of the problem. If you remember this, you'll help avoid blaming them or being triggered by whatever they might say or do, however inadvertently. (We discuss *Conflict Escalation Triggers,* and how to avoid them, in Part Three.) Instead, the real problem is that you have a need that isn't being met. So, what specifically is the need that is being threatened, or isn't being satisfied in that situation?

This isn't always an easy question to answer, especially when you're in the midst of a conflict and are flooded with emotions, thoughts, and judgments. As always, it helps to take a moment to pause and reflect. The more specifically you can identify the feeling, the more accurately you will be able to identify the need—and thus take the necessary steps to get that need met so you no longer have to put up with the negative feelings. But before we get to our discussion of strategies—i.e., how we try to meet our needs—here are a few tips to help identify the underlying need by first identifying the corresponding emotion with greater clarity and precision:

Tip #1: Differentiate between thoughts or judgments and actual feelings. Often we'll say things like, "I feel like you ignore my ideas," or, "I feel betrayed." Such statements don't really describe a feeling; ignoring ideas is an action, or a behaviour. Betrayal is also an action. Therefore, such phrases are judgments or thoughts about how the other person is treating you. In the heat of a conflict, a sentence like "I feel like you ignore my ideas" or "I feel betrayed" can easily sound like an accusation. That's why blaming feelings, as we like to call them, aren't very helpful. On the contrary, if they're expressed outwardly they can often worsen the problem by unintentionally escalating the conflict. No one likes to be accused of hurting someone else, intentionally or accidentally.

A quick test of whether your feeling is a genuine emotion or an attempt to find fault/lay blame is to check whether you can describe your feeling using only one adjective. If you can complete the phrase, "Right now I feel _____," with a single adjective (e.g., hungry, tired, angry, etc.), and the word you choose isn't just a verb in the past tense (e.g. ignored, betrayed, etc.), then it's probably an authentic feeling or emotion.

Another test is if you're drawn to complete the phrase with "like," "as if," "you (or he/she/they)," or "that," then what's likely to follow is not an authentic feeling. Examples might include "I feel as if you're ignoring my input," "I feel like he/she/you betrayed me," or, "I feel that I'm being judged," and so on. Instead it's likely to be a thought, judgment, or an interpretation of someone else's actions or intentions. Any one of the words in Figure 9 (among others) is probably an indication that what you're expressing is not an actual feeling but is instead a thought or judgment:

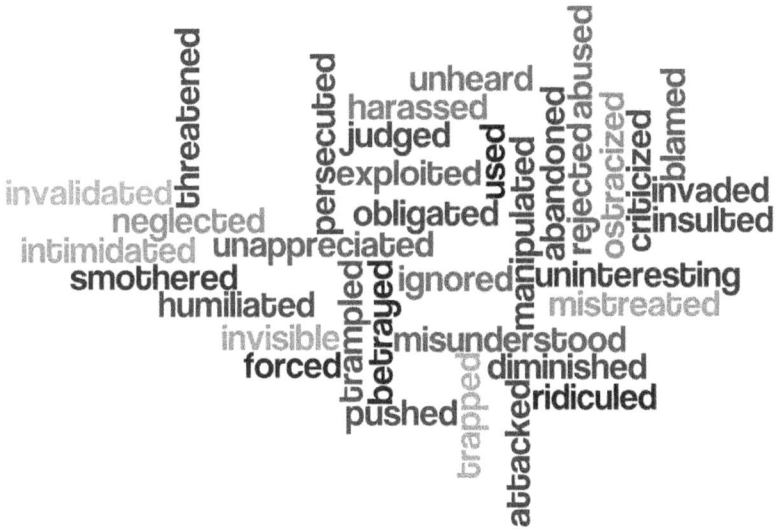

Figure 9: Blaming-feelings.

For example, "Right now I feel as if you're ignoring my input," "I feel like I'm being ignored," "I feel that you're not listening," or any variation on these themes implies that someone else's actions (and the intentions behind them) are the problem — in other words, your feelings are somehow their fault, their conscious, personal responsibility. Instead, the real underlying cause is a need that isn't being met, and it's bringing up these associations and emotions for you. True, their behaviour is related to that unmet need, but their intentions may be perfectly innocent or well-meant. As we'll explain in Part Three's analysis of Conflict Escalation Triggers, ascribing or imputing intentions should be avoided at all costs.

A more accurate, authentic feeling statement might be, "I feel frustrated about my input not being used," or, "When my ideas aren't used, I feel sad." Identifying the sadness (or anger, loneliness, disconnection, or whatever you're actually feeling) allows others to understand and empathize with what's going on for you internally, and gives you a platform for asking for what you need so that you no longer feel that way. Thinly veiled accusations will not be received so empathically.

Having identified frustration, sadness or loneliness as the real underlying feeling, you're now closer to identifying what you would need in order to no longer feel that way—for example, you might need to be heard, validated, acknowledged, or included as full-fledged member of the team.

Tip #2: Pay attention to the metaphors and language that you and others use, as they may contain helpful clues. As tricky as language can be, it can still be useful in pointing to the real underlying feeling. When in the midst of conflict and emotional turmoil, we sometimes resort to metaphors—phrases or idiomatic expressions that serve as replacements or illustrations for something else we may not be able to readily identify. So when in the heat of the moment someone uses a metaphor such as, "I feel like I was left in the lurch," or, "You left me holding the bag," what they're probably trying to tell you is, "I feel lonely," or, "I feel guilty." By decoding the underlying feeling of abandonment, guilt, or whatever it might be, you've basically recognized the unmet need—the need to feel included as part of the team, or the need to feel vindicated, etc.

Tip #3: Recognize that frustration is a generic feeling for any need being unmet, and try to dig one level deeper. If you can identify a feeling as frustration, then you already know a need isn't being met. The problem is that the feeling of "frustration" could just as easily apply to the need for freedom of artistic expression as to the need for sexual release; so while it's unquestionably a feeling (and not a thought or judgment), it's too broad a term to be very helpful in the immediate situation. The trick is to figure out exactly which underlying need isn't being met, so you can ask more specifically for what you need.

Try to remember what immediately preceded the feeling of frustration, because that will likely point to the underlying need. For example, if a feeling of frustration is immediately preceded by another person interrupting you, then chances are the real need behind your feeling of frustration is the need to be heard, uninterrupted (and/or to be respected, validated, etc.). If you feel frustration following a brainstorming session in which none of your ideas were acknowledged by the others, then you might be needing acknowledgement, validation, or some related feeling.

Tip #4: Recognize that anger is a secondary emotion. By this we mean anger is usually preceded by another, primary feeling, which again is the source of the real underlying unmet need. For example, if someone leaps out at you from around the corner of a dark alley and shouts, "Boo!" your first instinctive reaction is usually fear—but it quickly turns to anger, as soon as you realize your life isn't actually in danger. Your next instinct, instead of running away, might be to beat the other person up. This is a holdover from our primitive safety mechanism, which leads all animals to either freeze, flee, faint, or fight when confronted by a natural enemy. The anger is what manifests most powerfully, lasts longest, and thus what we remember most vividly, so we tend to identify it foremost as the feeling. But you can see how the anger is actually a backup response to one or more of the following primary emotions:

- surprise (unmet need: predictability, stability, safety)
- fear (unmet need: safety, security)
- hurt (unmet need: belonging, trust)
- etc.

Because anger so universally supersedes and masks other emotions, your initial emotional reaction to the person or situation is a better indicator of the real underlying unmet need.

Tip #5: Recognize that most needs in a conflict boil down to a few common ones. In a typical conflict situation, if you dig deep enough, you'll discover the underlying needs behind most unpleasant feelings are the needs for belonging and social status, safety or security, respect, acceptance, validation, acknowledgement, recognition, or support. That's not to say that all needs in a conflict can always be distilled down to just these few, but they are most common in workplace conflicts in particular. If you try a little practice and observation, you'll begin to see that most revolve around needing to feel like part of the team; to have one's authority or title respected; to be recognized for a contribution or (job) performance; to get help and alleviate the sensation of being overwhelmed; and so on.

To practice identifying the unmet needs in a conflict—whether yours or the other person's—fill in the blanks in Table 5 below. Examples are given in the first few rows, so, in light of what you've just learned about unmet needs, see if you can decode the underlying need for the last few rows:

If you "feel":	...then you might need:
1. Stupid	Validation, acknowledgement, recognition
2. Insecure	Security, reassurance, safety, stability
3. Confused	Clarity, decisiveness, calm
4. Ripped off	Fairness, equality, mutuality
5. Helpless	Autonomy, self-efficacy, safety, contribution
6. Stabbed in the back	
7. Worthless	
8. In the dark	
9. Left holding the bag	
10. Betrayed	

Possible answers: 6. *Feeling*: hurt, sadness, loneliness; *Need*: security, trust, belonging. 7. *Feeling*: sadness, disappointment; *Need*: self-worth, esteem, validation. 8. *Feeling*: insecurity, confusion, loneliness; *Need*: safety/security, clarity, inclusion, loyalty. 9. *Feeling*: loneliness, guilt; *Need*: togetherness/belonging, support. 10. *Feeling*: loneliness, hurt, sadness; *Need*: Togetherness, belonging, inclusion, support.

Table 5: Decoding feelings and needs.

This table is obviously not meant to be definitive or exhaustive; it is necessarily selective. *In more than one case, we deliberately threw you a curve by including some metaphorical language and/or some thoughts or judgments*, just to see if you could discern what the actual underlying feeling(s) and need(s) might be. That's why the first column's heading uses "feel" in quotation marks!

Note, too, that for each feeling – or thought, or judgment – there is a multitude of conceivable underlying needs, including ones not listed here.

Again, this is why we identify them as merely "possible" answers. There is seldom (if ever) a single "right" or "wrong" answer; the codes can often be interpreted in multiple ways. If a feeling or unmet need is difficult to pinpoint, either for yourself or another party, then part of your job is to ask the right questions to help you discover exactly what need isn't being satisfied.

Questioning is both an art and a science; it can be a delicate task requiring advanced skill, and one that is beyond the scope of this book. Suffice it to say that how you frame a question can make a significant difference in how well the other party responds to it. Consider, for example, that closed questions – ones that can only be answered with Yes or No, and typically beginning with the word "Did," "Can," "Are," and so on – can be easily perceived as controlling or directing the conversation, which may further frustrate or anger the other person. Open-ended questions that can't be answered with a simple Yes or No and beginning with words like "How," "Where," and "When," are generally better at inviting the other party to open up in dialogue. Be careful – even an innocent inquiry beginning with the word "Why" can be interpreted as a challenge.

Instead, we recommend trying open-ended approaches to help surface the underlying needs, similar to the following lines of inquiry:

- "Tell me what your concern is about."
- "Help me understand what is important to you about _____."
- "Tell me what you were hoping for with regard to _____."

If the other party has no idea what the unmet needs are (either their own or yours), it makes sense that they won't be able to satisfy them. They're not mind readers, and in the midst of the emotional storm, that's easy to forget. We often resort to our own frequently inelegant, awkward, or just plain backhanded strategies for meeting our own needs. The problem is that these poorly executed strategies tend to result in further bad feelings. For example, if one crew member is complaining about something, it may simply be that they only want to be heard, or they might be doing it just to engage in the conversation involving complaints – in other words, to demonstrate solidarity. But if a colleague keeps chiming in with solutions to the problem being complained about, it may only add to the complainer's frustration. Why? Because the complainer just wants to be heard, or be part of the crowd, and not necessarily have the problem fixed. That would alleviate their reason for being heard or showing sympathizing for the group. The complaining is really just a strategy to get something, and not necessarily a resolution to the apparent problem. (We analyze strategies in more depth in the next section.)

The trick to understanding each other (and staying out of conflict) is to identify and address the needs that each person is seeking to satisfy. As long as any one party to a conflict feels discomfort and has unmet needs, the conflict will continue. It's important to understand your own underlying needs, as much as the needs of the other person(s). If you know what you are working with in terms of needs to be addressed, it becomes much easier to talk together and build solutions that genuinely meet your own needs without threatening or negating the other person's.

One important feature of our human feeling-needs is that they are seldom (if ever) in conflict with each other. In other words, needs are always compatible. If this sounds incredible or counterintuitive, look at the list of needs in Figure 8 again. Can you find two needs that are irreconcilable? In other words, is trust fundamentally incompatible with or opposed to safety? Does one person's need for warmth negate the other's need to experience beauty? Does one party's need for joy necessarily deny another's need for a sense of discovery? What about compassion versus belonging, and so forth? If you go through the list you can see why it's entirely possible for two or more parties in conflict to each have their needs met without denying the other(s).

To be clear, the needs may exist simultaneously. For example, A may need recognition while B may need respect. Or they may exist in parallel, as when both parties need the same thing (for example, validation or belonging). Occasionally you may find yourself with the very same unmet need as someone else at the very same time. In fact, a common issue in arguments is that neither side feels heard or acknowledged by the other! The needs may even complement each other (for example, one needs to be heard, while another needs a democratic decision-making process), but they're rarely opposed. For better or worse, we all share these needs, and we all need to have them met, often at the same time.

It's important to stress that the needs themselves are never really in conflict. It's how we go about satisfying them that brings us into conflict. Fortunately, clever and creative folks like you can always find ways to satisfy the needs of the parties to a conflict. The trouble really arises between people when their strategies for meeting those needs are incompatible. Let's examine those strategies now and see why some of them work well while others don't.

The Role of Strategies

You now have a better understanding of feelings, needs, and how they function in conflict situations. From a conflict resolution perspective, feelings are simply a warning sign. They are necessarily positive and valuable, even if the emotions themselves are negative and uncomfortable. They should not be ignored or repressed. Instead, we should always pay close attention to them to figure out what information they give us about our needs. Needs, in turn, are simply the things we must get met in order to feel comfortable again and return to our normal, conflict-free state.

Strategies, then, are the actions we take or behaviours we exhibit in order to have those needs met. To take a simple example, defrosting a frozen pizza is one strategy to satisfy hunger; phoning in an order of Chinese food for delivery is another. So are hunting, fishing, and cooking. All are outward manifestations of the same inner need to eat.

Now consider the role of film and TV. In our culture, entertainment is probably as vital a part of your life as breathing, and so you may be tempted to think of movies as a need. But watching them, and writing or producing them, are actually behaviours and actions. By definition they are strategies, or approaches to solving the problem of meeting a need. So what need do these activities fulfill? They may meet your needs for joy, creativity, self-expression, freedom, inspiration, companionship, accomplishment, communication, or a host of other possible (and equally real) needs, including earning a living.

The problem is that strategies can run the gamut from the healthy and smart — like engaging in a creative outlet — to the dysfunctional and destructive. An example of the latter would include drink and drugs, strategies used by some to obtain an artificial high or escape unpleasant feelings. In a conflict-specific context, we adopt all sorts of strategies to get what we need in the moment. Unhealthy or dysfunctional examples can include everything from the passive (such as avoiding eye contact, remaining silent, refusing to participate), which meets our need to stay out of harm's way by avoiding conflict, to the more aggressive (including arguing, name calling, insulting, etc.), which might meet our need to win or to be right. Interruption can be a (dysfunctional) strategy for having our opinion heard. Between these two poles are strategies we might call "passive-aggressive," like insisting, "No, I'll be OK, we can move on," when clearly all observable signs, like a terse tone of voice and arms folded across the chest, suggest otherwise. Like the other strategies, these passive-aggressive approaches are intended, subconsciously at least, to deliver some sort of result and meet a need. Passive-aggressive behaviours may meet a need to feel righteous or to obtain some high moral ground ("Don't mind me, you look after yourself, and I'll just suffer here quietly!") while simultaneously avoiding the discomfort of conflict. The manifestations are as diverse as the range of their possible underlying needs.

Again, most of us aren't even aware that we are employing these strategies, because they happen at a subconscious level. They're more or less automatic. The problem is, we're seldom taught to decode them properly. We tend to accept them at face value. As with conflict resolution skills in general, most people have never learned how to "read" strategies – either our own or others' – and interpret them for what they are. We rarely pause and reflect before interacting with each other in ways that are non-dysfunctional and non-destructive. Instead, we act instinctively and impulsively, using whatever strategies have worked for us in the past—however clumsy and unsophisticated they may be.

Infants offer a useful analogy here. Babies cry when they are tired, get stomach gas, or have dirty diapers, because they haven't yet developed language to express their need to sleep, be burped, or have their diapers changed. Babies are not conscious of using a strategy when they cry; they may not even be fully aware of the unpleasant feeling that caused them to invoke it. All they know is that they're uncomfortable and they need help to fix the problem. Crying seems to work; it usually evokes a rapid response from Mom or Dad, so naturally that's what they do. It becomes their default strategy.

Despite our relative mastery of language, adults aren't much more advanced. Our feelings trigger the same old strategies because they seem to get us what we need. They're reliable, if blunt, instruments, and they've successfully kept us going as individuals and as a species. Even though our brains are much better developed than our ancestors', our basic repertoire of responses has become so hardwired into our genetic programming that we never question it. It just works! Our primitive problem-solving approaches boiled down to some variation of fighting, fleeing, freezing, or fainting. In many ways, modern humans have evolved far beyond that, or so we like to think. But in truth our instinctive responses, actions, and behaviours often resemble fighting, fleeing, freezing up, or playing dead (fainting). If we feel a need to be validated, our strategy might be to argue our viewpoint until we are acknowledged as being right. We may even continue to push for as long as the desired response isn't obtained, indefinitely if necessary. If we feel a need to belong to the tribe, we will clam up or run away to avoid being ostracized. If we feel a need to have our opinion heard, we will yell or slam doors until someone finally hears. Like babies, when we need something, we tend to just act out, using the first available strategy without immediately worrying about its negative consequences.

As in more primeval times, any threat to our physical safety or security is met immediately with the old "4-F" response. But our emotions react just as quickly (and crudely) to any perceived threat to our mental or emotional well-being, too. Our bigger brains are highly evolved to deal with the greater complexity of modern life and its concomitant challenges. Many of our basic biological and safety needs are met, and that frees us to cope with more abstract and higher-order needs. This includes threats—real or imagined—to things like our self-concept or identity. So if a director reacts to an actor's performance in a way that shakes the latter's self-image as a brilliant and versatile talent (for example), that psychic attack can be felt just as powerfully as a real, physical one. A person whose physical safety or security is threatened will fend off an attack or retaliate, and a person whose need for esteem or self-realization (for example) is somehow threatened will also react defensively. The only real difference is that in the latter case, the reaction will probably take the form of words instead of fisticuffs.

To illustrate, let's revisit the case of the cast or crew member who shows up late to set. The First AD's emotional VU meter is crossing the threshold because they feel that their own time isn't being valued or respected by the latecomer, or perhaps they feel their authority is being challenged. Their strategy for meeting the need to feel valued and respected is, like the underlying feelings and need, also in obscure code. So they might greet the latecomer with a glare and bark, "You're late!"

To the First AD's subconscious mind, such a heavy-handed response is a quick, easy way to assert authority or dominance and thus gain the desired respect. The problem, of course, is that such an impromptu strategy is likely to be met with a commensurate defense—or more accurately (since this is an emotional rather than physical attack), defensiveness. Lather, rinse, repeat: a cycle of attack and counter-attack is initiated, and before long the production has a full-blown internal conflict on its hands.

Again, in the heat of the moment we seldom allow our larger, more advanced brains the time—mere milliseconds, really—to pause, decode our feelings, figure out what the unmet needs are, and simply ask for what we need in the calm, polite way we would normally expect of modern *Homo sapiens*. As Viktor Frankl once wrote, "Between stimulus and response there is a space. In that space is our power to choose our response." In that space, we can thoughtfully respond—not react!—in a way that is more highly evolved and helpful than the instinctive fight-or-flight mode. Instead of barking an accusation and setting off a vicious cycle that might lead to further disarray on the set, the First AD from our example who (justifiably) needed to feel respected and valued could have simply engaged in productive dialogue about his needs with the tardy cast or crew member. A calm and mutually respectful discussion would have been a much better choice, a much more effective response. Part Three contains many tools and techniques for making these intelligent decisions.

When we learn to talk with each other at the level of our needs, it's much easier for us to understand each other and develop more effective, successful approaches for satisfying them. The problem, though, is that most of us have only learned to interact with each other at the level of our strategies, letting our actions and behaviours do the talking instead. Most of our strategies are dysfunctional: I bark at you; you bark right back at me. Every ill-considered action or reaction is just as likely to deny or frustrate the other person's need as it is to temporarily and superficially meet our own:

"You're late again!"

"Oh, yeah? Well, talk to my union rep!"

If actions speak louder than words, and our behaviours are inelegant and inarticulate, it's no wonder we have conflict. Without the training to respond differently, we will continue to react in our instinctive, inappropriate ways. So if what someone is doing or saying sets off your feelings VU meter, you are likely to react accordingly and jump straight into strategies—just like the barking, glaring First AD in our example — in a ham-handed attempt to protect or satisfy needs that are being threatened or unmet, without even consciously recognizing what those needs are. When people react negatively to someone's strategies (i.e., actions/behaviour), they are doing so because those particular strategies are perceived as threatening or somehow violating their own need(s).

Before moving on to analyzing other examples, we'll take a quick step back, because we've only decoded half of the interaction. We know the feelings and needs of the First AD. If actions and behaviours are the outward manifestation of an unmet need, then what about the strategies of the latecomer? What unmet need is being addressed by the action or behaviour of showing up late?

It's hard to say without being able to ask the right questions, of course, but in this hypothetical example it's possible that the cast/crew member's tardiness is a way to exert control. Perhaps the call time was set without his approval or input, or perhaps the revised call sheet was simply never received, setting off fears of being left out. Unconsciously, then, our cast/crew member might have decided to assert the need for a sense of control by leaving the house at their own discretion, and not when the First AD "dictated" they should leave. Or it could simply be that leaving the house late was a way to satisfy the need for more time spent doing something else at home. Either way, showing up late is itself the unintended result of an unconscious strategy.

Previously, in our discussion of needs, we classified wants as desires – that is, nice to have, but not critical to one's well-being and emotional health. We also described them as being code for strategies, which we now know to be covert ways to satisfy the more crucial unmet needs in a conflict. So let's connect the dots between these ideas.

Suppose there is a conflict involving one or more unmet needs. This will inevitably trigger strategies to meet the need(s). The strategy, or strategies, applied by the parties to the conflict are likely to lead to prolonged conflict, as long as the core need(s) remain unsatisfied. So far, so good – we understand the interplay between these mechanisms.

But what if one party has fear of conflict? Perhaps the anxiety is due to a history of family violence, or a desire to protect the relationship from further damage. In this case, a second strategy of avoidance may kick in.

This avoiding behaviour allows the person to dodge any feelings of discomfort, albeit temporarily. So in this example the avoidance offers temporary relief from the fear of conflict, and may even feel necessary for the person experiencing it, but it won't actually resolve the original issue or meet the primary, underlying need. Instead it just prolongs the agony. It's only by facing the conflict and working it out with the other person that the original need can be met. Thus, you can see how avoidance is a strategy for getting something else that the person might *want* – namely, a respite from the fear or anxiety – but doesn't ultimately *need*. That can only be done by having a difficult conversation and handling the original problem.

Strategies, then, don't really satisfy the primary, underlying needs. At best they're superficial responses that meet short-term wants, and they seldom stick. In this particular case, the avoidance strategy serves a second-order need, or more accurately the *desire*, to sidestep the discomfort of the conflict. Temporarily averting the pain is nice, but it doesn't address whatever it was that sparked the conflict in the first place.

Feelings, needs, and strategies in a conflict can be multilayered, so it's extremely useful to practice analyzing and decoding these interactions. Let's look at a few more examples that we can break down into the possible feelings, needs, and strategies experienced by the parties. Conflicts can get far more complex, especially when they begin to spill over and involve others, but we've kept the examples below relatively simple to illustrate the core concepts. Note that in each case we list only some "possible" feelings, needs, and strategies, because we are analyzing the situation based on observable phenomena alone. It's premature (and potentially dangerous) to assume that our interpretations are correct, especially without asking the right questions and getting good, accurate information in response. It does, however, highlight the array of possibilities that one might need to address in even the most basic conflict situation.

4: INT. BOARDROOM - DAY.
CHRIS and ROBBIE are writers drafted in to punch up a big budget romantic comedy. This is not their first team effort, but it's the first time rescuing another writer's work and not creating something original from the ground up. It's also the first time they have started to experience palpable tension between them on a project, possibly because it's someone else's work, the value of the picture, or their distaste for the genre.

Normally each perfectly complements the other in terms of what they bring to the script, and each can usually count on the other to come up with ideas to fill in any dramatic or comedic gaps; their disparate personalities allow them unique perspectives on the characters and plots they develop. This time, there is sniping and bickering far beyond the good-natured ribbing that characterizes their usual collaboration. The judgments and put-downs of the other's suggestions have led to screaming matches and walk-outs, and the occasional hurled object, depending on the partner.

If Robbie and Chris were to prepare to sit down and work out the issues causing damage to their relationship, here is what they might see:

Person	Strategy	Possible feeling(s)	Possible need(s)
Robbie	cajoling, criticism, put-downs	anxiety, inadequacy, discomfort with genre	familiarity, confidence, control
Chris	criticism, shutting down, silent treatment	anxiety, inadequacy, discomfort with genre	familiarity, confidence, control

Table 6: Scene 4 - feelings, needs, and strategies.

5. INT. SOUND STAGE - NIGHT.

As the studio teacher in charge of child welfare, TAYLOR's first responsibility is to the child actor. Strict rules require that minors can only work a maximum number of consecutive hours, with or without breaks. This is not to say that there is no loyalty to the rest of the cast and crew. In fact, it has been a fun and mostly low-stress production, although in the last week or so there have been increasingly late call times due to the union minimum turnaround times required.

On more than one occasion DALE, the First AD, has pushed the shoot right up to (and even slightly over) its maximum legal duration and has given Taylor a frosty reception, perceiving the studio teacher to be the obstacle to greater productivity. Taylor has had to politely but firmly remind Dale of the letter and spirit of the law protecting the child actors, and Dale has consistently countered with comments such as, "One more shot won't hurt." Dale takes the role of the director's right arm very seriously and wants to make sure that any momentum is preserved and actors remain firmly in character until the director calls cut for the day. Taylor wonders if the First AD's increasingly confrontational attitude has begun to infect other members of the crew. Already considered to be lowest in the pecking order, Taylor senses that others no longer sit at the same table during breaks or chat as readily as before.

If Taylor and Dale were to recognize each other's behaviours as calls for help, and then sit down and discuss the situation, here's what they might find:

Person	Strategy	Possible feeling(s)	Possible need(s)
Taylor	assertion	loneliness, isolation, disrespect	recognition, support, team membership
Dale	commandments, orders, "triangulation" (enrolling third parties in conversations)	job anxiety, deadline stress, loyalty (to director)	relief (from time pressure), loyalty (from Taylor), recognition, respect

Table 7: Scene 5 – feelings, needs, and strategies.

6. INT. PRODUCTION OFFICE - DAY.

CASEY, a young writer-director, was fresh out of film school and coming off a major win at a prestigious indie film festival. One thing led to another, and soon a studio offered the highly touted Casey a one picture, multiple option deal with a moderate budget. The expert crew assembled for the show was second to none and had decided to rally around the director to provide the best possible support on Casey's first major production, sure to be a stressful one for a relative newbie. That is, until an anxious Casey showed up and started laying down the law. Whenever considered professional advice or opinion didn't coincide with Casey's vision, the director snapped at the unlucky bearer of inconvenient feedback. Soon the entire cast and crew had transformed from willing supporters into reluctant employees. GENE the production manager was faced with a possible mutiny as one by one colleagues filed into the production office to lodge complaints about unfair and unwarranted treatment at Casey's hands. For now, Gene is reluctant to confide in the producer lest it cause disappointment, but time to act is running out.

If the parties to this deteriorating situation could sit down and discuss the situation a little more calmly, this is what they might discover:

Person	Strategy	Possible feeling(s)	Possible need(s)
Casey	Micromanagement, autocratic rule	insecurity, disrespect	security, control, confidence, support, respect, validation
Cast & crew	third party "triangulation," complaints, working to rule	resentment, mistrust, confusion, disrespect	trust, acknowledgment, recognition
Gene	avoidance	frustration, loneliness, stress	support, assistance

Table 8: Scene 6 – feelings, needs, and strategies.

Again, in each of these scenarios it's important to remember that the Possible Feelings, Strategies, and Possible Unmet Needs listed here are only best guesses as to what may be going on for each of the parties involved. The Strategies are the only real, visible artifacts in each interaction, the only objectively observable phenomena. It's impossible to say with certainty what any of this really means until and unless everyone acknowledges their actual, underlying feelings and explicitly identifies their unmet needs. Even then, you will often find that people aren't sufficiently in touch with their feelings and needs to be able to name them. (You may be one of those people.) *The most important thing is to remember that the strategies, however annoying or frustrating they may be, are really just attempts to express a need.* They're not so much about you, as they are about them. Even so, you are now better equipped to help the other party (or parties) meet those needs in some way.

What's interesting about the first case (and possibly others) is that the parties may actually have similar feelings and sometimes the exact same needs, yet their strategies are very different. As with our previous analogy illustrating the wide variety of available strategies to satisfy a hunger, there are many ways our covert strategies can be designed to meet needs. Rather than see themselves being in opposition to each other, people in conflict should stop to explore just how closely aligned they often really are.

Back to Ones: Summary

In this section, we examined how feelings in conflict situations act as an early warning system, alerting us to unhealthy situations or perceived threats or challenges. We now know the meaning and purpose of a range of feelings relating to conflict: frustration, for example, is what we feel when a need isn't being met; anger is a subsequent but equally natural reaction that energizes us to fight for something that is important to us; and so forth.

Most of these feelings relate to real human needs in the midst of conflict. People need to feel valued, respected, heard, and other common sentiments. This, of course, is helpful in order to understand our own motivations and feelings, but if we can gain insight into the needs of the other party in a conflict situation, it gives us tremendous leverage in finding creative ways to meet these basic needs without having to sacrifice or compromise our own needs at the same time. It costs nothing to acknowledge and give credit to the other party, for example, or provide reassurance of some sort.

The problem is that most of us remain unaware of these needs, and in conflict situations we usually choose a means to help us satisfy them in an equally unconscious fashion. A strategy is simply an approach to a particular problem; most of our instinctive ones are effective but crude – useful in the short term, but more damaging to the relationship in the long run. The instinctive logic of feelings, needs, and strategies works something like this: "Something happened and it caused me pain, therefore this must be some sort of attack, and therefore I must lash out to stop you. If I hurt you as painfully as you wounded me, you are likely to quit hurting me." This reasoning self-perpetuates and leads to a downward spiral of aggression and attack, defensiveness and counter-attack.

One way to help keep things from deteriorating is to speak from our own experience, but in order to do that without lashing out, we need to know the difference between authentic feelings and blaming feelings. An authentic feeling statement is, "I feel angry"; a blaming feeling statement is, "You make me angry." The former expresses ownership of the emotion, whereas the latter attributes causation to the other person. Sometimes we use metaphoric language, as in, "I feel stabbed in the back." This is bound to sound more like an accusation to the other party (someone had to do the stabbing), and we shouldn't be surprised if the other person dismisses, denies, or deflects it and counters with an accusation of their own.

Now that we have a solid foundation in understanding the inner mechanics of conflict, we'll continue to explore ways to prevent conflicts from happening in the first place. We'll also learn how to manage and resolve them more effectively, without escalating them or having them devolve into open warfare.

PART THREE:
ESSENTIAL CONFLICT PREVENTION AND RESOLUTION SKILLS

Learning outcomes: By the end of this section/chapter, you will have the skills, knowledge, and attitudes necessary to

- apply two Guiding Principles of conflict prevention and resolution; and

- use a checklist to ensure you follow all four steps to conflict resolution (do a Perception Check, synchronize Intent and Impact, use "I" Statements, and follow the 5-step Fifth House Creative Conversations Model).

The Way to Conflict Resolution

By now you should have a better-than-average understanding of how feelings, needs, and strategies work (for better or worse) in conflict situations. Next, you will learn the fundamentals of successfully navigating a conflict situation. If you stick with the principles described here throughout the conversation(s) and follow each step using your newly acquired skills to the best of your ability, you greatly increase the likelihood of an outcome that will benefit both you and the other person(s) in the conflict.

Even so, it's hard to overcome a lifetime of bad habits, replacing them with good habits overnight, so there may be quite a bit of deprogramming and reprogramming that has to take place in order to resolve or manage conflicts well. That's OK; skills take time to develop. The important thing is to do your best and remember that people will almost always respond positively when they see, hear, and experience a sincere attempt to fix an uncomfortable situation. It's likely that if you are not happy about the situation, the other person isn't, either, so they will probably appreciate your initiative and welcome the opportunity to resolve the issue. Good leadership involves modeling the behaviour you seek.

You'll notice Part Three – the book's "money shot" – isn't much longer than the preliminary stuff. That's because there are many excellent books, videos, courses, and other in-depth resources on how to work through a conflict, and some are found on (or linked from) our website. If or when you have the inclination, time, and opportunity, we certainly recommend that you make use of them in order to increase your knowledge and enhance your skills. In the meantime, our goal here is to give you what we consider to be the absolute, must-have basics. We're keeping it short and simple in the belief that the less "technique" you have to learn, the sooner you'll get past the conflicts, build confidence, and increase your conflict management ability.

Before we begin, there are two Guiding Principles to be applied throughout any discussion aimed at conflict resolution. These Guiding Principles are fundamental to preventing or resolving conflict. If you keep them in mind and observe them at all times during a difficult conversation or conflict situation, you will greatly increase your likelihood of a successful outcome: *Avoid the Conflict Escalation Triggers*, and *Always Use Active Listening*.

Both of these are explained in detail in the section below. Once you're familiar with these and have practiced using them, you will be far better equipped to step into conflict resolution. There are four basic steps to conflict resolution: Do a Perception Check; Synchronize Intent and Impact; Use "I" Statements; and Follow the 5-Step Fifth House Creative Conversations Model.

Each of these four steps will be covered in turn, beginning with the Perception Check, but first we must explain our two Guiding Principles.

Avoiding Conflict Escalation Triggers

Imagine a production whose creative principals have different creative visions for the show. This difference is not going to automatically generate a conflict, just like having different political views, religions, or ethnic backgrounds won't necessarily create a problem. Differences exist everywhere we look and can often be used to foster even greater creativity. To reiterate, research suggests that a healthy amount of vigorous debate, disagreement, and dialogue is necessary to coming up with the best possible outcomes, if it means all ideas are well-dissected, analyzed, and "battle-tested." Furthermore, those engaged in the discussion are more likely to support the outcomes, because they feel satisfied that it's the best, most robust solution. The trick, then, is to allow for the differences without letting them lead to a conflict – or at least, ensuring that the conflict remains productive and not destructive or dysfunctional. The good news is that this is possible, even likely, because it's entirely within the power and control of those involved.

The bad news is that there are specific triggers that can almost guarantee that disagreements will escalate into conflicts if one (or more) individual is tempted to pull them. We describe them below.

However, if you know what these tripwires are, then there are already two things you can do to prevent conflict from breaking out: First, not allowing yourself to be activated by the triggers. Second, not using them to provoke others. The deliberate choice to avoid the Conflict Escalation Triggers, coupled with some basic communication skills (beginning with Active Listening, described in a subsequent section), will set you well on the road to having a productive conversation with a positive outcome.

Let's now identify these Conflict Escalation Triggers and explain how conflict escalates when they are used. Understanding the triggers means knowing what *not* to do.

Trigger #1: Using the word "You," followed by blame, accusation, exaggeration, or insult when having a discussion about something on which you disagree. In a disagreement, you might begin talking about an issue, but it becomes a conflict as soon as the word "you" is used, at which point the discussion becomes about a person. In other words, the focus of the conversation shifts from what is wrong with the relationship or the situation, to what is wrong with the other individual. When people hear the word "You" or its variants at the start of a sentence, they are primed to expect that what follows next is invariably some sort of accusation, judgment, or other personal attack. For example: "This is your fault!" (blame), "You're being irresponsible!" (accusation), "You never listen to me!" (exaggeration), or, "You don't know what you're talking about!" (insult).

Imagine yourself on the receiving end of any of these statements. When attacked, it's normal and natural for a person to become defensive and then go on the counter-attack. As discussed with regard to feelings, needs, and strategies, this is as true of verbal assault as it is of the physical variety. As soon as someone feels under attack, the conflict escalates from a disagreement to what we call *personalized conflict*—because it has become personal. The conflict is no longer about the issue that needs to be fixed; it's now about a person. The situation has just been made worse, and so there are hurt or angry feelings to deal with in addition to the original problem.

Let's look at a typical difficult conversation, one that is still focused on fixing the person or judging them as bad or wrong instead of fixing the problem. Notice what happens when the word "You" is used. In the following everyday situation, observe how quickly the conversation between John and Jane degenerates as soon the latter enters the room:

JOHN
(*Understandably upset.*) You're late! Call time was twenty minutes ago.

JANE
(*Defensive now, accused of holding up production.*) It's not my fault. The driver was late. [Shifting of blame.]

JOHN
(*Increasingly frustrated, due to apparent lack of responsibility and failure to apologize.*) Transport captain said he waited for you for twenty minutes before you walked outside! You should have gotten up earlier, or at least called.

JANE
(*Getting more upset at being ordered what to do.*) Oh, right, like you're perfect, John? You're acting like you're the boss of me! [Return accusation.]

...and so the downward spiral continues.

Bottom line: by all means, attack the problem—together—but never attack the person. When involved in a difficult conversation, stay focused on the issue at the center of the disagreement. Only use the word "You" to start a sentence if it is followed by something neutral, positive, or a compliment. This is a conscious choice you will have to make if you want to keep the situation under control and prevent it from getting worse.

A better way to handle this particular conversation would be to wait for a calmer, cooler moment to bring up the issue. By pouncing on Jane immediately when she enters the room—no doubt already feeling flustered, guilty, or expecting to be shamed—she isn't in the best head space to have a trouble-free conversation. Calling her out in public can only cause more embarrassment or shame, compounding any defensiveness she may already be feeling. Taking her aside later, the best difficult conversation starter would be some sort of neutral observation. For example:

JOHN

(*Privately, after table read.*) That was a good rehearsal! Now, Jane, I'd like to take a minute to talk with you about today's late start time to see how to prevent it happening in the future.

JANE

Yeah, I'm sorry about that. My driver was late. [Shifting blame.]

JOHN

(*Taking the blame-shift in stride as a normal way for Jane to discharge the unpleasant guilt feelings.*) I appreciate your apology. What can be done to make sure we can start on time from now on, in case traffic is worse than anticipated?

Notice that John avoids inflaming tension by, first of all, starting on a positive note, and then by avoiding blame or judgment. He also successfully avoids triggering Jane by speaking from his own perspective and acknowledging her apology. John also reiterates what Jane says, demonstrating that John was paying attention to Jane rather than preparing some sort of speech, attack, or other response. John then invites Jane into a problem-solving dialogue rather than unilaterally imposing a solution, which is bound to backfire. The entire time, John carefully avoids using the word "You" in a negative way, particularly at the start of a sentence. As soon as that happens, Jane will likely stop listening. But John avoided the trigger, and she remained open to dialogue.

When stuck in a personalized conflict, what typically happens is that as the level of emotional stress increases, the parties take it up a notch with the next trigger.

Trigger #2: Proliferating the issues. This means starting off talking about something specific but suddenly adding another issue—generally something equally contentious—into the mix.

This commonly happens when one brings up a problem from the past or introduces an unrelated issue to the one under discussion. To borrow the previous example, if John and Jane were trying to address the issue of starting rehearsals on time, Jane might proliferate the issues by saying something like, "Yeah, well, I heard from another crew member that you always used to show up late, too." While the counter-claim of lateness may appear related to the original problem, it isn't; it dredges up history. The comment is not focused on the immediate problem and, worse yet, it also involves gossip that may be unfounded. It certainly doesn't help the current situation. A common reaction to such a statement would be defensiveness, denial, explanations, angry retorts, or counter-attack by John.

Note that it could just as easily have been John putting another unrelated issue on the table. Imagine an exasperated John, trying to address the issue of punctuality, suddenly adding, "You know what else I don't appreciate? You're always bringing your girlfriend to the set. This is a closed set, not a social club!" With that he has just plopped another largely unrelated issue into the conversation. Again, the situation is ripe for devolving into personalized conflict. Eventually, "an eye for an eye makes the whole world blind," as the saying goes…all because one person gives in to temptation and uses Trigger #2.

Proliferating the issues is a sure-fire way to escalate conflict. Most of us can probably relate to this scenario: an argument with someone that starts off being about something relatively benign turns to upset and yelling, and soon neither party can even remember how the whole thing started. How did you get to this point? Quickly and easily! A simple disagreement, with both parties trying to work it out in a reasonable way, transforms into personalized conflict when one uses the word "You." Then someone digs up the past or introduces unconnected complaints, further escalating the situation into *destructive* or *dysfunctional conflict*. It's called destructive or dysfunctional conflict because it's here that things really start to fall apart, and teams or groups start to lose their ability to perform at their best.

There is still one more trigger that is guaranteed to make things even worse than they already are.

Trigger #3: Talking to others about what happens between you. By "talking to others," we don't mean trying to get some help or coaching about how to repair the situation; that would be an acceptable, helpful form of side-conversation. Instead we mean essentially gossiping or seeking sympathy from someone other than the persons directly involved in the conflict.

Some call this "triangulating," because it introduces a third person into the drama. Others might call it "blabber-mouthing," "feeding the rumour mill," or "running to Mom and Dad/the Boss/etc." Another term is "forum shopping," when we keep turning to others until we finally obtain the desired sympathy. Whatever you prefer to call it, the problem is that the people in conflict start talking to outsiders about the other party (or parties) to the conflict — instead of talking with or to each other. In doing so, the person using Trigger #3 is effectively making the choice to escalate a conflict that has already gone past the personalized stage and has been pushed to the destructive stage. By taking it even further, it has leveled up to what we call *hostile conflict.*

You probably know from your own experience that the purpose of talking to outside parties about the conflict, and about the people involved in it, is generally to convince the third party that our point of view is right and justified. In telling the story to others, we usually portray ourselves as the innocent victim of an injustice or perhaps the avenging hero. In either case, according to the old fairy tale paradigm so familiar from childhood, if we are the hero or the victim then logically the other person must be cast as the villain. As the victim, hero, or both, it's easier to feel righteous about a position. We can use it to attain some higher moral ground, to be used as leverage in the argument. In telling these dramatic tales, we are trying to get others to choose sides in the conflict—preferably ours, and not the other's.

If and when this happens, those people newly enrolled in the drama will then typically talk to more outsiders, and they in turn talk to others, and so on. Consider the last time you were embroiled in your own conflict drama. How many people that you enrolled actually respected your plea to not tell anyone else? Probably very few. Most went straight to someone else to share the juicy story. "You'll never guess what s/he said/did to so-and-so…" Before long, all sorts of people get involved and misinformation, warped perspectives, and unfair judgments abound. The result can be a big, ugly mess.

Not surprisingly, by the time a conflict reaches the hostile stage, it becomes quite difficult to resolve without some sort of intervention. This is because more people are now involved in the original unresolved conflict, and this additional complexity creates group dynamics that are tricky to manage. And for many of those dragged into the conflict, the whole matter starts to become about saving face rather than about actual problem-solving and conflict resolution.

Let's go back to our previous sides and see what happens when it escalates to the hostile conflict stage and additional characters are drawn into our original minor drama starring John and Jane:

CHUCK

(To John.) Wow, Jane is really ticked off at you. Did you really threaten to fire her for being late?

JOHN

(Stunned by the surprise comment, defensive at the veiled accusation of dictatorship and by the betrayal of confidence.) Where did you get that idea?

CHUCK

Jane told me herself.

JOHN

(Temper rising.) And you believe her? That drama queen! She's always pulling this crap.

CHUCK

(Now defensive because John thinks he's gullible.) Hey, don't shoot the messenger, I'm just telling you what I heard.

89

JOHN

(To Dave.) Can you believe Jane? She went crying to Chuck, trying to gang up on me!

With each additional conversation, and each new person pulled into the conflict, more fuel is thrown onto the fire. Left unchecked, it can develop into *polarized conflict*, which is hostile conflict taken to a whole new level, with battle lines clearly drawn and factions formed. Communication typically breaks down and the parties to a conflict take sides. Polarized conflict can split productions or entire studios, networks or agencies apart. The examples contained in the introductory section on the history of conflict in film and TV were just a random sampling of the most egregious.

This scenario paints a gloomy picture, but take heart: you have just learned the three most important things to avoid doing if you want to prevent conflict from escalating or keep it from starting in the first place. Refuse to use the triggers.

If you can successfully avoid having your own buttons pushed by them or pushing someone else's, you'll have an enormous amount of control over the situation. You'll be better positioned to create a positive outcome whenever you are faced with a difference or disagreement, even if it has escalated to a higher level of personalized or destructive intensity. Take a good look at the illustration in Figure 10: Conflict escalation and triggers. It shows how quickly and easily conflicts can escalate due to the use of triggers, often unintentionally. Commit it to memory, and start using this knowledge the next time you feel yourself reacting.

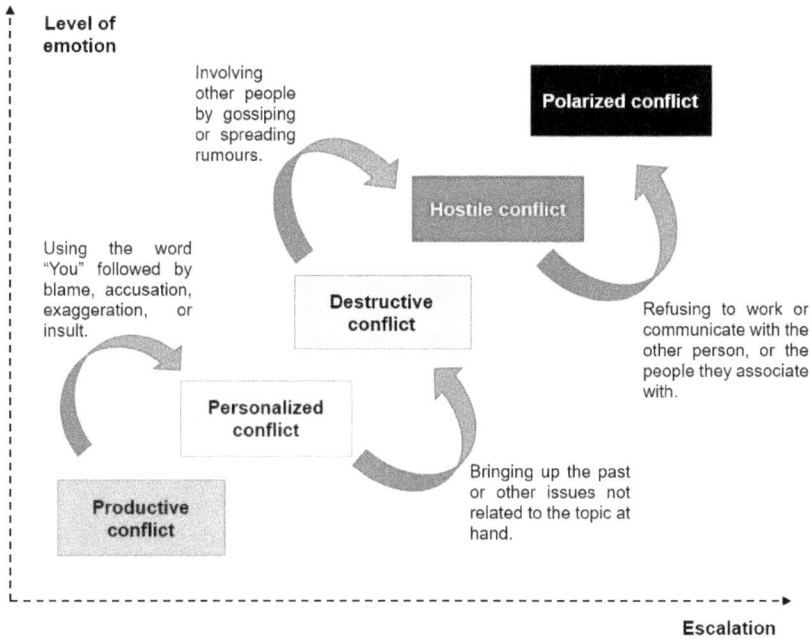

Figure 10: Conflict escalation and triggers.

Key point: You can control the outcome of a difficult conversation by ensuring that you do not give in to the temptation to use the triggers. Like responding thoughtfully versus reacting emotionally, it is a choice. Choose wisely and you will be delighted and amazed with the results, especially as the heat of the conflict reduces to a manageable level and others take their cues from you.

On that note, it's also important to remember that even while you consciously choose to avoid these triggers, it doesn't necessarily mean that the other person(s) in the conflict won't be using them. Unless they have the same knowledge and skill set that you are now developing, it's possible—perhaps likely—that you will encounter these triggers in a conversation, particularly when the other person's feelings are engaged. People use triggers all the time without even realizing it. They may not be doing it intentionally, and probably aren't. When it happens, your job is to avoid taking the bait and to rise above it. Few have the necessary training or practice, so you need to take the lead. Ignore at all costs any "You" statements directed your way, no matter how much they sting, or else you will find yourself triggered. Keep the conversation focused on the issue, the thing that needs to be fixed. Never retaliate.

You can help the other person in a disagreement reduce or eliminate their use of triggers by demonstrating how it's done. In setting a positive example, you can help them recognize their own button-pushing, whether it's deliberate or accidental. For example, you could say, "Zoe, I just heard you say, 'You're always doing this and that.'[5] I'd prefer not to discuss the past right now. Let's stay focused on the present, which is how we are going to resolve the current issue. If you want, we can come back to your concerns about what it is that I'm always doing, if we can get the original matter dealt with first, OK?"

The next time someone tries to proliferate the issues, stay calm and focused. Recognize it for what it is, i.e., a covert strategy to satisfy some unmet need, however unclear it may be to you. For example, Zoe's frustration might be compounded if she thinks her counter-attack didn't have the desired effect of putting you on the defensive. In that case she might follow up with another attempted proliferation. As painful as that kind of comeback might be, resist the temptation to strike back. Your job is to lead the other person to a less confrontational, more satisfactory result.

Therefore, since it's your choice what happens next, an appropriate response to Zoe's last shot could be something like, "OK, so we now have three things to work out: the original issue we were discussing, the second issue you mentioned a moment ago, and now this other subject. Realistically, we can't talk about everything at the same time, so let's finish our conversation about the first issue. We'll see how long that takes and afterwards decide on when we should talk about the other two." In a way, successful conflict resolution is like fighting a fire: the best way to avoid a conflagration is to deprive it of more fuel.

It's worth repeating that unless you are in the enviable position of having a disagreement with someone of equal conflict resolution skills and knowledge, you will probably run into the triggers. Refuse to be drawn in. Instead, make a conscious decision not to engage in any of the three triggers yourself, even when they are being used against you. They almost certainly will be. Again, absent any other training in conflict resolution skills, people resort to the only available strategies they know will provoke a reaction (even if it's not the best, most productive kind of reaction). The

---

[5] Note the Active Listening technique, addressed later in this chapter.

use of Conflict Escalation Triggers is a coded form of admitting, "I feel guilty [etc.] and I'm really uncomfortable about this. I need you to truly understand what I am feeling right now, so I'll have to push your buttons until you feel as bad as I do, too!" Triggers almost always get the wrong kind of results, and unfortunately they're guaranteed to get attention—which is why people keep using them.

Rather than allow yourself to internalize the hurt and risk retaliation, the best way to show you got the point is to empathize. Simply acknowledge and validate the other person's pain. "Zoe," you might say, "I really get that you're upset by this. I'd probably be upset, too, in this situation." By exercising the choice to avoid triggers yourself, you will always end up in a better position than if you had reacted to them. Afterwards, you can always go elsewhere to let off some steam, decompress, and shake it off, because preventing conflict from escalating is hard work. It's good work, and necessary, but it is challenging and requires strength and stamina. Make sure you reward yourself for it.

Dramatis Personae: The Five Conflict Response Roles

No discussion of conflict in film and television would be complete without a mention of the roles its participants play. We all act out a particular part when we find ourselves in a conflict, whether we realize it or not. There are no scripted lines, but each role does have a specific, predictable pattern of behaviours that distinguishes it from the others. Each interacts with the others in particular, predictable ways.

Here, we are no longer talking about the classic hero-victim-villain paradigm discussed earlier. Those are different, self-designated roles that we consciously and subjectively assign to claim the moral high ground or, conversely, to objectify the other person as the "bad guy." The roles we are discussing here are not based on the presumed guilt, victimhood, or avenging righteousness of the parties, as seen from our self-interested point of view.

Instead we refer to five common conflict response roles that are assumed by all parties to a conflict. For the most part they are adopted subconsciously (although they can and should be used consciously wherever possible). They are objectively observable and, to the extent that we can accurately assess our own beliefs, attitudes, and behaviours, they are even measurable. The five conflict response roles are based on clusters of characteristics that are consistently exhibited by each of these roles when in conflict.

In no particular order, we call the five roles Moderator, Decision-Maker, Loner, Diplomat, and Friend. The theory behind the conflict response roles is that each of us responds to conflict in a particular way, consistent with one of these five roles, according to the extent to which we prioritize certain values. These can be mapped to a two-dimensional graph (Figure 11), with the vertical (or X) axis representing the extent to which we focus on ourselves, the facts of the situation, and the task or process at the heart of the conflict. The horizontal (Y) axis represents the degree to which we focus on the other person or people, the relationships between those involved in the conflict, and their feelings. Because these are relative values, we can all locate ourselves somewhere on the spectrum. Each person's response to conflict will be somewhat different than another's, although people sharing the same role will typically respond in a broadly similar way. Their exact measures along the two dimensions may vary, but general patterns of behaviour can be seen in each of five basic conflict response roles (see Figure 11 below).

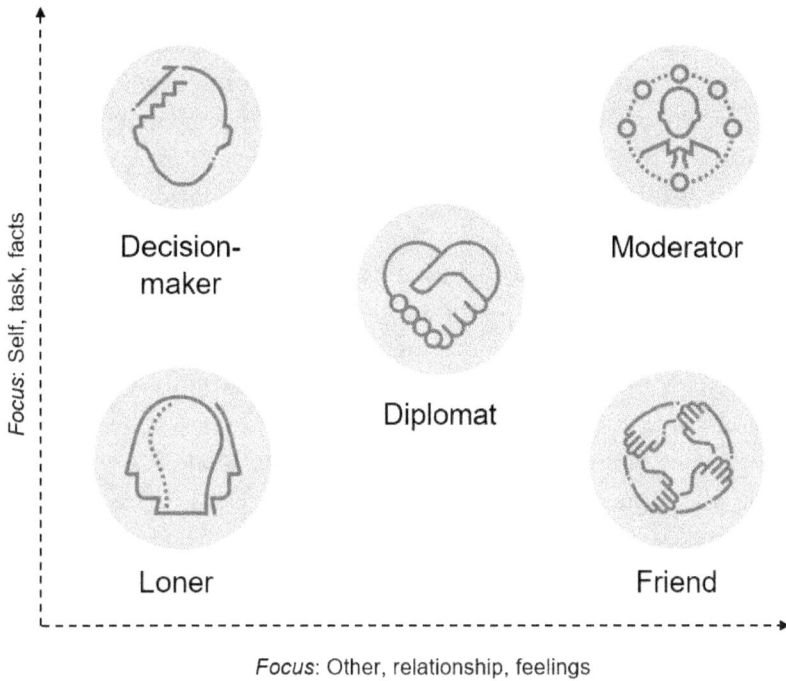

Figure 11: The five conflict response roles.

In time and with careful observation you may learn to identify another's conflict response role based on the behaviours they exhibit. As this book was being written, the authors were struck by this description appearing in The Hollywood Reporter's obituary of the late, Canadian-born director Arthur Hiller (*Love Story*, *The Out-of-Towners*): "[He] was a flexible craftsman, bringing out the best in writers and actors he collaborated with…perhaps better known for his diplomatic skills than for a distinctive directorial vision. But that diplomacy served him well when working with several strong-willed actors and writers; he was always willing to subordinate his own personality to the talents of his collaborators."[6] In the absence of other identifying features, this could easily apply to the role of Diplomat, whose style is to seek compromise among those in a conflict. That said, it might also apply to Friends, who tend to subordinate their own needs to the needs

---

[6] http://www.hollywoodreporter.com/news/critics-notebook-arthur-hiller-hollywood-920495, accessed December 15, 2016

of others in conflict in order to preserve the relationship. Regardless of exactly which conflict response role Hiller typically occupied, it still can tell you something valuable about what's most important to him (or someone like him) when in conflict. Since both roles are found in the middle to lower right quadrant of the matrix, Hiller probably prioritized the needs of the other person(s), the relationship between the people involved, and/or their feelings.

A detailed analysis of all five Conflict Response Roles is beyond the scope of this book, but you can learn more about them on our website at www.fithhousegroup.com/cr2i . In the meantime, it will help to remember that one factor that can cause conflicts to be so stressful is how our own conflict response role(s) may interact with another's. Friends, for example, have different priorities and needs in a conflict than Moderators. Relatively speaking, the former are generally much more interested in preserving the relationship and the feelings of the people involved in the conflict, whereas the latter will typically prioritize the problem-solving process and thus be more interested in gathering data and input from the parties. As mentioned earlier, these two sets of needs aren't necessarily incompatible, but in a conflict, stress might result from the fact that Friends might simply be anxious to smooth things over quickly, while Moderators might prefer to patiently seek further consultation and input. You can see how Friends' behaviour might frustrate Moderators, and vice versa, especially when emotions are already running high.

Be aware, too, that the roles and their associated behaviours always have consequences when in conflict with another. Even two persons who share the same default role – in other words, under most normal conflict situations they adopt the same cluster of behaviours that characterize their shared role – will interact in a particular way that can cause additional stress and frustration. Imagine, for example, how two Decision-Makers might behave when both value winning the argument, or two Loners, who might both aim to avoid the conflict. You might think those with the same conflict response roles would have an easier time understanding each other, but a conflict between them can be just as painful as any other (if not more so), and can be unnecessarily prolonged.

Sometimes, when we find our default role isn't working, we often subconsciously shift into our secondary or tertiary roles as required. This means we are not rigidly stuck in one set of behaviours every time we get into conflict. Instead we are versatile, adopting other backup roles if the situation demands it, usually because our needs and priorities aren't being met by our primary or secondary roles. This has its advantages, but it can also cause frustration when it's perceived as inconsistency or unpredictability by the other party.

There are two things to take away from this. The first is that the roles we play in conflict inform our behaviours, and these behaviours are strategies designed to meet our needs or priorities. That's all. We simply differ in what those priorities and needs are, and how we try to satisfy them. The second is that if we understand how we respond to conflict in these roles, and how others respond, it will give us more tools for mutual understanding and ideas about how to adjust our interactions to make them more satisfying when in conflict.

In addition to learning more about conflict response roles at our website, you can also find an online self-assessment tool called the Conflict Response Roles Inventory (CR^{2}I)™ that will help you identify your primary and backup conflict response roles, in case you haven't already identified where you are on the conflict response roles spectrum.

The Power of Active Listening

Regardless of where you might currently find yourself on the conflict continuum, whether you think trouble might be brewing or if you're already right in the thick of it, one thing is certain: your single most powerful disarming and de-escalation tool will be your ability to listen.

Imagine a situation where you are in the early stages of a conflict. Perhaps you are upset with someone. You are worried, or suspicious, that they might have done something, or are about to do something, that would have a negative impact on you. So you muster up the courage to say something, because you really want to make sure everything is all right between you. You start telling them what's on your mind, when they interrupt you. They take over the conversation with one of the following responses:

- their version of the facts ("No, that's not how it went, this is what actually happened…")
- their denial of what you were saying ("No way, you can't be serious

— is this some kind of a joke…?")

- their feelings about what you were saying ("Hold on a second, I'm not OK with this, you are totally out of line…")
- their dismissal of what you were saying ("How did you come to that conclusion? That's just ridiculous…")
- etc.

If that's their best answer to something you are trying to fix or figure out, chances are it doesn't feel good. If anything, it feels even worse than when you first broached the subject. You can probably appreciate what it's like not to be truly heard, never mind understood.

The reality is that few ever listen with full attention. Even at the best of times we devote only a few spare brain cycles to listening. When we're in a conflict situation and our blood is boiling, our pulse is racing, and our mind is reeling, it's even less likely we're listening. Instead, if we really tuned in to our thought patterns, we'd notice that we're busy doing other things. There's a whole other inner conversation taking place. Mostly we're trying to "read between the lines" to find hidden meanings, interpreting (or misinterpreting) signals, and/or composing our response to what's being said. In most conversations, we're mainly waiting for our turn to talk instead of truly listening. This is particularly true in conflict, when we're more likely to be reacting to triggers and preparing justifications, rebuttals, or counter-attacks.

Now imagine that an individual you are trying to converse with keeps quiet and listens to you intently. Every time you speak, the only thing they say is, "Go on," or, "I see," or just, "Uh huh." They periodically check to make sure they understand what you're saying. They don't add anything about themselves, reality-check you (i.e., present an alternate interpretation of events or facts), or insist on their opinion or viewpoint. They give you all the time you need to fully express yourself, and when necessary they periodically confirm their understanding with you. They say things like, "If I understood you correctly, you feel…" followed by a close restatement of your own words. How would you feel then? Much better, no doubt.

Listening actively means turning off the interior chatter, offering occasional encouraging nods or sounds, and refraining from interruption. It also requires occasionally reframing, restating, or rephrasing what is actually heard in order to check and demonstrate genuine understanding. It also involves giving the speaker opportunities to correct any misapprehensions or misinterpretations. Being able to accurately reflect back to the other person what they're saying proves to the other person that you are taking them seriously. It demonstrates that their perspective is important to you. It shows them that you truly care about what they think and what they are experiencing.

Anyone on the receiving end of this novel treatment, who feels that their perspective is important and that they matter to you, will feel safe, at least on a subconscious level. They will feel heard and respected regardless of whether or not you agree with them. And therein lies the power of Active Listening: if someone feels safe and respected, you can pretty much count on them to be willing to get through a difficult discussion and want a positive outcome as much as you do – even if you still fundamentally disagree. Conversely, anyone who feels threatened, unheard, disrespected, or almost anything else will always be more interested in defending, justifying, or attacking. Or running away.

An active listener makes for a good role model. Eventually the other party will make the connection between how good it feels to be heard properly and how much better the conversation goes as a result. With a little luck and encouragement, they will try it, too. It may not go perfectly at first; at times you may need to ask them for the same consideration in refraining from interruption, for example. But with Active Listening, an otherwise vicious cycle can be turned into a virtuous circle of clearer communication and improved collaborative problem-solving. If you want to fix something with someone, it's wise to help them get into a head space where they will want to fix it with you, too. That way you ensure the best possible outcome for yourself, for them, and for the situation. Of all the strategies to employ in a conflict situation—consciously or unconsciously – Active Listening is by far the most effective at moving the conversation forward and reducing the emotional heat.

Why is Listening So Difficult?

The power of listening is critical, but the reality is that truly hearing what other people are saying is challenging even at the best of times. There are many reasons for this, all of them legitimate. Here are just a few:

We think at 400-500 words per minute but speak at 125-150 words per minute. This means that in the sixty seconds it took one person to say only a couple of sentences, the other person's mind and thought processes are already racing far ahead, simply because that part of our brain works that much faster. By the time one party can get their first two sentences out, the other has already begun to do any or all of the following:

- interpret the other person's words, body language, tone, intentions
- decode the other's strategies and other covert signals, either consciously or subconsciously, and accurately or inaccurately
- judge their position, reasoning, motives, assumed motivations, etc.
- evaluate all of the above, deciding whether it's "good" or "bad," "truth" or "lies," and a host of other possible conclusions

We are susceptible to distractions. Active Listening demands that we focus on the speaker and on what they are saying, and it means that we aren't doing anything but that. The only allowable exceptions are the small interjections that we might offer in order to demonstrate attention, encourage the speaker, and show understanding of what is being said ("I see," "Yes," "Go on," etc.). There is an endless array of distractions, and you know from your own day-to-day experience that we are constantly bombarded with them. A partial list of common distractions would include:

- incoming texts, phone calls, email, or social media messages
- any other ongoing issues or concerns (such as relationships, work, school), whether related or unrelated to the current one
- physical sensations (such as hunger, feeling tired, medical issues, hangovers)
- visual distractions (TV, people, animals, scenery)
- body language, facial expressions
- background noise
- etc.

We have expectations and assumptions. If we go into a difficult conversation already expecting the other person to receive us in a certain way, act a certain way, or say certain things, we will be looking to confirm those expectations. We'll observe how they speak and behave, then interpret it so that it lines up with our predictions. It's human nature to collect evidence to support our belief that what we anticipated is correct. We are pattern-seeking, meaning-making beings. The psychology literature calls this common problem "confirmation bias." In other words, we are predisposed to seeing patterns that prove us right—even if those patterns aren't actually there. It may comfort you to know that this well-studied phenomenon doesn't just happen to people in conflict; it can happen to everyone in all kinds of situations. Even scientists researching alone in their labs can be susceptible. We are more sensitive to what we expect to see or hear, and we tend to tune out most other information. This means we are not hearing everything but are instead selectively filtering out the information that doesn't fit with our mental image or expectations.

Expectations are dangerous because they can easily turn into self-fulfilling prophesies. For instance, let's say that a production meeting has been called by Janice, who is the Production Designer. Tom, the Art Director who has been experiencing some friction with Janice lately, figures that he will either be sacked or at least have the riot act read to him by Janice. As he makes his way to the meeting room, he is having a different kind of rehearsal in his head: fueled by his expectations, Tom is preparing arguments to use against Janice and is thinking about venting all his pent-up feelings and frustrations. With every step, he is working himself into a state of righteous anger. By the time he reaches the boardroom, he's primed to explode at the slightest trigger, however inadvertent.

But for all he knows, Janice may simply want to try out her newfound conflict resolution skills, perhaps discuss possible materials for set decoration, or maybe make an announcement that only indirectly has to do with Tom. Because he anticipated the worst, when he walks in with a scowl and the other key production team members greet him, he hears everything as either sarcasm, pity, or condescension. If someone asks, "What's wrong?" out of genuine interest, Tom responds with unnecessarily cutting comments and pretty soon the situation devolves from a potentially happy outcome into a loud, sustained argument, culminating in Tom's impromptu firing.

"See?" he exclaims. "I knew all along that you guys just wanted me out."

Tom gets to be right about his expectations—but he's far from happy about it. To avoid this outcome, always check your own expectations and, when necessary, ask yourself: would I rather be right or happy? Remain open to being pleasantly surprised.

We often go into difficult conversations assuming we know all the facts, have all the information, or know what the other person is about—we've already "figured them out." Assumptions in this situation act much like expectations: we are waiting to observe or hear things from the other person that only serve to validate our assumptions. Anything that doesn't agree with our predetermined ideas gets filtered out, and thus a lot of opportunity for true understanding is lost.

For example, Robin might notice that Dan is withdrawn and uncommunicative in rehearsal. There are all kinds of things Robin might assume from Dan's behaviour: Dan is mad. Dan is bored. Dan is in character. Dan doesn't care. But in truth Dan might have received some bad news from home shortly before showing up to rehearsal. Maybe Dan is having money troubles, or he split up with his significant other.

Robin could simply ask Dan what's wrong and why he's not his usual, outgoing self. But if this were a conflict situation, it wouldn't be so simple. We commonly attribute other people's behaviours to motivations that aren't necessarily true. The reasons seem plausible to us because that's how we might behave ourselves if we were feeling the way we assume the other person to be feeling, based on their perceived behaviour. Robin assumes Dan is withdrawn and uncommunicative for the same reasons she might be, but of course that's not necessarily the case.

Needless to say, this can rapidly inflame an already tense situation. In a conflict, a simple unanswered phone message, text, or email could be taken as a sign that the other person is angry, doesn't care, or is trying to punish another party — although it could just as easily mean that their smart phone battery ran out of power. If Dan suddenly snaps at Robin, Robin might attribute that to something she had said or done to offend Dan. But it's just as likely that seconds earlier Dan was thinking about an overdue bill or the fight with his partner. If Robin automatically assumes that it's directed towards her—which she's likely to do if there's already any tension between them—then responding in kind will just escalate the situation. Always test assumptions, beginning with your own.

Active Listening is a skill that must be learned and is seldom innate. While some people are uncannily good listeners, we generally have to learn the skills to listen actively. One false assumption that makes listening surprisingly difficult is that we must be naturally adept at listening just because we're born with ears that never shut off even while sleeping. Avoid conflating hearing with listening.

Active Listening requires a particular set of competencies and constant practice, application, and refinement. It's not enough to learn the words in the script; you have to repeat them over and over in order for your dialogue to sound sufficiently fluid and natural. Even then, you might need to try different readings to get the best results. Listening, like acting, lighting, or cinematography, can be a process of trial-and-error. And the only real way to judge how adept you've become is to try it out and wait for the results.

Those of us with a natural talent for Active Listening can still improve by consciously developing the skills, getting feedback, and incorporating what they have learned – especially in conflict. Even with dedication, perseverance, and a few lucky breaks, only a certain percentage of filmmakers or actors ever become professionals, but anyone can become a good active listener with enough practice.

We believe it is more important to speak than to listen. This should come as no surprise for most of us, because this is how we've been programmed since childhood.

As youngsters we are rarely taught conflict resolution skills by our parents or caregivers. Conflict is typically handled through some sort of disciplinary measure, such as time-outs, punishment, and so forth. A voice of authority puts an end to most arguments. When we enter grade school, conflict resolution skills are still not part of the curriculum. Once again, conflict between students is typically dealt with by authority figures meting out consequences, as opposed to some form of genuine collaborative problem-solving. By the time we get to high school, we experience more of the same, even though we have more advanced problem-solving and decision-making skills. Things do shift a bit, though: we may find that conflict goes underground, to be dealt with surreptitiously. It might take the form of shaming, shunning, bullying, or harassment. It's often about getting the last word or being the loudest.

Sadder still, upon graduating and entering the workforce, we find that the "adult" approach to conflict isn't much different. Now the authority figure is the boss, and the consequences are typically fear of reprisal or job loss. It is still relatively rare for employers to ensure that employees receive training in conflict resolution skills in the workplace, even though it's very much in their interest to do so. But why should work communications be any different from the rest of our public interactions?

Even our democratically elected governments, which we consider the hallmarks of a civilized society, invite more talking than listening. Political debates are the primary method of dealing with differences in policies or ideologies. Just like school, our houses of government celebrate and reward argument or rhetorical ability, far more than they value skills for genuine dialogue. All things considered, the fact that most people don't have conflict resolution skills is not a reflection of who they are as human beings but rather a reflection of what society prioritizes.

We are preparing our commentary or rebuttal. Due to the same kind of socialization, when in conflict we automatically default to the "I'm right, so you must be wrong" setting. This basically ensures that when we stop speaking, we rarely hear our counterpart, but instead compose a follow-up. If we happen to be in agreement, we are typically preparing to comment on that point of accord. As such, we are not actually listening to understand; we are really listening to highlight what we disagree or agree on. Crucially, seeing the other party as an opponent rather than a partner in solving our mutual problem is another major obstacle to listening.

Clearly, then, genuine listening does not come naturally to most of us. Real listening takes effort, and some of that work includes reprogramming and learning new skills. However, in doing so we equip ourselves with what is probably the most powerful ability in human interaction. You can imagine how hard it would be to stay angry and remain in conflict with someone who is clearly doing their best to listen, to genuinely understand you, and make room for your point of view. Listening is very seductive and disarming, and it will almost always put you in a position that will greatly increase the possibility of a successful outcome to a difficult situation.

How to Demonstrate We Are Listening: Essential Listening Skills

Active Listening is the second Guiding Principle of conflict resolution. As with the first principle (avoiding the Conflict Escalation Triggers), it's critical to exercise the principle of Active Listening from beginning to end in any difficult or conflict situation. Make a commitment to listen to the best of your ability any time you are trying to prevent a conflict or resolve one. If necessary, take a time out until you are able to listen with full attention. You will have to prove to the other person(s) that you are listening to them for two key reasons: First, they need to know you are being sincere and want to have a genuine dialogue with them. If they suspect you just want to keep scoring points, they won't listen, either. Second, it's an effective strategy for giving them what they might need to feel safe and comfortable, and to help reduce the levels of stress and anxiety in the conversation and in the relationship.

Note that Active Listening doesn't necessarily mean you have to like the person you're dealing with. That's just a fact of life. And while you won't always be able to achieve agreement, you need at least to be able to understand each other's perspectives. If you're going to work with them in any capacity, now or in the future, you can't afford to have conflict get in the way.

You can prove that you are listening actively by using three basic techniques: Paraphrasing, Summarizing, and Empathic responses.

Paraphrasing. Paraphrasing is repeating back to the speaker what you have just understood them to say, but in your own words. You do not repeat back to them the exact words of what they just said, which is parroting and can be interpreted as mockery or sarcasm. Instead, paraphrasing proves to the speaker that you have been listening because they are hearing a close reiteration of what they have just expressed. Subconsciously they will conclude that you must be listening, otherwise you wouldn't be able to accurately interpret what they just said. Thus, paraphrasing validates for the speaker that you are taking them seriously and not just selectively hearing what you want to hear (i.e., fulfilling your expectations) or twisting their words to fit your own agenda.

It's good practice to wait until they have made their point before you begin. Never interrupt, or it will just lead to more frustration. Sometimes it's useful to start your paraphrasing with, "What I heard you say was...," or, "What I understood from what you said was...," or similar wording. This signals your desire to check your understanding of their point of view rather than just reinforcing or reframing your own.

For example, let's say John is upset that Jane is late for rehearsal again. The conversation might go thus:

JOHN

I really hate it when you're late because the rest of us are always here on time. We have to make sure we leave our homes and jobs in enough time to get here for rehearsal, but for some reason you don't do that, and it makes me feel like you don't care about us as much as you care about yourself and the stuff you have to do.

JANE

What I heard you say is that you are upset that I don't value your time because you make more of an effort to arrive on time, whereas I don't.

JOHN

Yeah, I guess that's what I'm saying.

Notice that Jane wisely ignores the hyperbolic use of "always" (and its implication that Jane is "never" or "seldom' on time). Instead, Jane focuses in on the real underlying truth of what's being said by John. She restates the core elements of what John is saying but in her own words. It's not exactly what John said verbatim, but it's a close approximation—minus some of the more inflammatory rhetoric.

If you happen to misunderstand what is said or misrepresent what is intended, paraphrasing allows the opportunity for the other person to clarify or correct before any further miscommunication develops. It's human nature to want to be understood, and the other person will not hesitate to amend a paraphrase or restatement that is not in line with what they said. For conflict to be resolved, there needs to be good understanding and clarity between you as you work through a conflict.

It's possible that when they hear you paraphrase they will realize that what they said is not really what they meant, or maybe your paraphrase wasn't entirely accurate. Either way, simply restate what you hear them saying as they reframe or clarify their original statement(s). Keep doing this from a place of genuine curiosity until they're satisfied that you truly get what they're saying. It won't work if all you're doing is deliberately misquoting them in order to make them look bad or feel guilty! The goal is comprehension. There's no question that it requires patience and practice, but, once again, paraphrasing enables deeper understating between individuals.

Let's take a second look at the example, but this time let's say that for some reason Jane doesn't quite nail the paraphrasing the first (or even second) time. Maybe Jane focuses on the wrong thing, or allows emotions to get in the way and finds it hard to resist the temptation to be defensive. The same conversation might go something like this:

JOHN

I really hate it when you're late because the rest of us are always here on time. We have to make sure we leave our homes and jobs in enough time to get here for rehearsal, but for some reason you don't do that, and it makes me feel like you don't care about us as much as you care about your own time and the stuff you have to do.

JANE

What I heard you say is that you have concerns because you're always here on time and I'm not.

JOHN

No, that's not what I meant. Look, we all have stuff outside of rehearsal we have to do, but at least we're making efforts to get here on time, and you don't seem to have the same commitment.

JANE

What I understood you to say was that you don't believe I have the same commitment.

JOHN

No, that's not it either. I think you're committed to the project, but you don't operate on the same schedule as the rest of us and it pisses me off.

JANE

Ah, OK. What I get out of what you just said is that when I show up late you feel I don't value your time as much as I value my own.

JOHN

Yes! That's it.

See how much better that turned out?

Summarizing. Summarizing is the skill of helping to make a person's point for them. Sometimes, when people are really worked up, they lose some ability to be articulate; it's hard for them to choose just the right words to express themselves. Perhaps they're angry and their brain is overwhelmed with adrenaline, they're hyperventilating and not getting enough oxygen, or they may be so energized that they carry on for a while. Either way, to recap effectively, you simply listen through everything that they are saying, and then, in your own words, feed back to them what you understand to be the gist of what they are saying.

Summarizing is typically used when too much has been said to properly paraphrase, usually because the speaker is venting. When people rant, they often repeat one or two main themes, and perhaps throw in other examples or side issues, to reinforce their point. Summarizing what they are saying, as with paraphrasing, is validating; the person who is upset will feel that they've been heard and taken seriously. This will help them to move forward in the conversation. Again, summarizing accurately proves that you are listening to them, and this can only help.

Let's look at another scenario to demonstrate the skill of summarizing:

RON

I don't see why you should get an equal Executive Producer credit for this picture when I pulled most of the financing together and broke down the script to come up with the preliminary budget. I found the director and put most of the producing team together. You came in later and helped package the star, which I could have easily done myself through a casting agent or using my own contacts! You're worrying about the little things like whether craft services offers gluten-free items on the menu, while I'm always scrambling to solve the bigger problems! I don't see why you deserve the same credit just because you found the script.

LOU

What I understood you to say was that I don't contribute equally to the producing work.

RON

OK, you see? Now you're getting it!

The magic of paraphrasing and summarizing is that when the other party feels like they've been heard and understood they feel less of a need to keep making their point, which in turn reduces your need to make counterpoints, and so on.

Notice that Lou doesn't necessarily agree to what Ron said, but he does acknowledge it. There's an important difference.

Empathic responses: Of all the listening skills, empathy is probably the most powerful. It is similar to paraphrasing or summarizing, except that instead of reflecting back to the speaker the content of what they have said, you are reflecting back the feeling behind what they are saying. The focus is taken off the words and is instead shifted to the emotional content.

Empathic responses take listening to a deeper level and thus provide even stronger proof that you are really hearing the speaker. This is because you have to go beyond interpreting what the speaker is saying—that is, the external or surface story—into the inner, unseen emotional territory. A skillful empathic response demonstrates to the speaker that not only do you understand what they are saying, but you also understand what they are feeling. As mentioned before, try to imagine staying in battle mode with someone who is clearly demonstrating that they care enough to not only get what you are saying, but also get what you are feeling. Here we should stress that understanding someone does not necessarily mean that you agree with them! Strategically speaking, however, if you want to get somewhere in a conflict, you will go a lot further, a lot faster, if the other person feels heard and understood. Often when we're uncomfortable about their feelings, our instinct is to dismiss, invalidate, or minimize them, which is guaranteed to make things much worse.

Let's revisit our previous examples. This time instead of paraphrasing or summarizing, we'll show how the conversations might sound when empathic responses are used:

JOHN

I really hate it when you're late because the rest of us are always here on time. We have to make sure we leave our homes in enough time to get here for when rehearsal starts, but for some reason you don't do that, and it makes me feel like you don't care about us as much as you care about your own time and the stuff you have to do.

JANE

So this has all become really frustrating for you.

JOHN

Well, duh. Wouldn't you be frustrated?

JANE

I would be, absolutely.

If the other party in the conflict is reassured that you "get" them, emotionally speaking, then once again they won't need to try as hard to make you feel their pain—literally or figuratively.

Here's our second example, this time using empathic responses to connect and to validate the other's feelings:

RON

I don't see why you should get equal credit as Executive Producer when I pulled most of the financing together and broke down the script to come up with the preliminary budget. I signed the director and put most of the producing team together. I'm trying to put out a million fires while you're off doing who knows what.

LOU

So from what I understand, you feel this is not a fair situation for you.

RON

That's an understatement! How's this for not fair: you send me the script, leaving me to break it down and pitch it to investors, only showing up after I've done ninety-nine percent of all the groundwork. You're worrying about the little things like whether craft services has gluten-free items on the menu, but I'm always left to handle the bigger problems!

LOU

The way things are going have been really disappointing for you.

RON

During pre-production you said you were busy on another project, but the rest of us are managing to juggle our slates just fine! I don't see why you deserve the same credit. Maybe you started the company and it's your script, but the rest of us do a lot of the heavy lifting, too! You shouldn't automatically get the same credit.

LOU

I hear there's a bunch of things that are really upsetting for you in all of that.

Again, although it's frequently hard to find the right words in the midst of the emotional turmoil of conflict, it's worth the practice and the effort. Resisting temptation to rebut, argue, or interject with your own feelings is also difficult. If you must assert your own point of view in a discussion, the best thing you can do is be mindful of your framing and language; subtle signals can be powerful. Again, notice that despite all the empathizing, summarizing, and paraphrasing, Lou doesn't need to actually agree with Ron.

We recommend that you get into the habit of replacing the word "but" with "and." This slight change of phrase signals the possibility that both points of view may be valid, and both can coexist peacefully. Notice the difference between these two statements:

a) "I understand you think the second act should be changed, but I think we should keep it as it is and rewrite the third."

b) "I understand you think the second act should be changed, and I think we should keep it while making changes to the third act."

The word "but" in statement A effectively dismisses everything that precedes it. In other words, the second part of the sentence—the speaker's opinion—basically invalidates or overrides the first. In this sense the speaker is elevating his opinion over the other person's. The fact that the speaker thinks one thing effectively negates the other's opinion on the matter.

Notice in statement B that the word "and" suggests there are two truths—the speaker's and the other person's—and neither is lessened or overruled by the other. All it really does is juxtapose the two points of view without privileging one over the other. It invites the possibility that both perspectives are valid, they can coexist, and it reduces the likelihood that the other person will feel that their viewpoint has just been overruled or invalidated.

Here we suggest borrowing from one of the main rules of improvisational comedy: the principle of "Yes, and." In improv, actors must simply accept whatever truth is presented to them by the other actor(s) in a scene, no matter how absurd or unlikely it may be. The goal is to take what is given and build on it, using it to move the plot and action forward. To deny it or shut it down is to try to control the scene, which generally results in bad comedy. A similar idea applies in conflict: it's wisest not to argue or fight whatever reality the other person presents, even if it doesn't line up with your own. To avoid getting bogged down in further conflict, accept it – *you don't necessarily need to condone or agree with it!* – as long as you use it to make something bigger and better with it. Move forward and avoid staying stuck in arguing your positions. We'll address how to use all input most effectively to arrive at potential solutions shortly.

Preventing or Addressing Conflict in its Early Stages

There are four steps to conflict resolution. While practicing the two Guiding Principles of conflict resolution (i.e., using Active Listening and avoiding the Conflict Escalation Triggers), ensure you take each of the four following steps:

1. Do a Perception Check.
2. Synchronize Intent and Impact.
3. Use "I" Statements.

4. Follow the 5-Step Fifth House Creative Conversations Model.

Let's examine these in detail. Keep in mind that whenever you want to resolve a conflict, you should follow all four steps in this order—don't skip any, and don't switch them around. This will increase your chances of a successful outcome.

Step One: Do a Perception Check

Before attempting any conflict resolution work, check and make sure that what you think is going on is actually happening. We tend to perceive a situation according to our mental models of how the world works, and reality may be different. We might believe, for example, that someone who raises their voice does so only because they're angry, when it might simply mean they have a blocked ear and can't hear themselves very well. We often employ these "perceptual filters" to screen out information that doesn't conveniently match our internal stories or expectations.

All too often we allow ourselves to be unduly affected by events or actions when seen through the lens of prior experience. For example, a production team member might have been excluded from the decision-making process on a previous show and so they may fear a recurrence of that situation. If the same person isn't consulted on a given decision, no matter how trivial, it could be interpreted as a sign of trouble when the oversight or omission might was really just a result of haste or carelessness.

Remember, these perceptions or impacts tend to be more about us and our interpretations than about something that the other party in the conflict has actually said or done. In other words, before sitting down with the other party (or parties) to iron out a perceived conflict, make sure there really is an issue. In some cases, you will be pleasantly surprised to learn that the source of your concern was a simple misunderstanding.

Checking your perceptions is therefore the first vital step in successful conflict resolution—and sometimes it can also be the last one. When we check our perceptions, it is quite possible there is no real problem. ("No, I'm not mad at you at all! I just got into a near-accident on the way to set, and I'm still shaking.") So before launching into the hard work of listening and exercising your conflict resolution skills, just make sure all of that energy and effort is warranted. This reality-testing is known as a Perception

Check.

Be careful! A Perception Check can go sideways quickly if not handled well. There are three constituent parts to a Perception Check:

a. Describe what you are noticing.
b. Ask what it means.
c. Turn judgment into curiosity.

Let's break these down. The first sub-step is to *describe what you are noticing*. At this stage, something has happened or something was said that doesn't sit well with you. Your emotional VU meter is trembling. Rather than sweeping the issue under the rug, hoping it will go away and risking a buildup of resentment, you go into conflict prevention mode and address what is bothering you. What was it, exactly, that was said or done (or not said or done) that troubles you? Without attaching any interpretation at all, describe the situation to yourself. Describe the "it"—the *what*—and not the *who*. (Remember to avoid the Conflict Escalation Triggers!) Write your perceptions down.

Avoid any inflammatory or judgmental words. Don't use any of the unhelpful communication methods, like exaggerating, minimizing, or criticizing. (See the sidebar under The Five Steps of a Fifth House Creative Conversation Model for more tips on avoiding unhelpful communication.) Using neutral words, describe what was said or what happened in such a way that any bystander would agree is factually accurate.

You could say, for example, "I noticed that a decision has been made about the order of today's set-ups." This is a far more factual, objective, and neutral description of the situation than, "What the hell is going on here? Did you guys deliberately not let me have any input on the order of the set-ups?!"

The latter may be a more accurate reflection of your inner state—your thoughts and feelings—and in that sense is subjectively "true," but it can't be independently verified by a casual observer. The inflammatory language, accusations, etc., may be evidence of how you feel, but they don't actually describe the situation itself. The goal here is to accurately capture the words, actions, and other visible, external artifacts of the situation. Internal things like feelings and judgments or thoughts aren't helpful at this stage. You'll address your feelings and needs about the situation eventually. A neutral observation will set the conversation off on a much better footing than the personalized, emotionally charged interpretation.

A conversation that starts neutrally invites a response equally free of negative vibes, for example, "I realize it may look that way, and we didn't intend to leave you out. We were just trying to adjust for the updated weather forecast calling for rain this afternoon."

Perhaps just by doing the very first part of a Perception Check— describing what you are noticing—it will clear the air and prevent a conflict. The other party now understands that you might be upset because of how you perceived something, and they can help clarify the situation. There's no longer an issue.

On the other hand, starting off with an interpretation—especially one that turns out to be incorrect and an accusation—is much more likely to provoke a defensive reaction along the lines of, "Hey, relax! You got it all wrong—how could you even think that?!" Before the conversation started, only one party was upset; now there's two. It was an unnecessary conversation that started and ended badly, when it really didn't need to take place at all.

Let's assume your inquiry was greeted with something like, "Yes, that's right, we discussed the set-up order after we wrapped last night, and you weren't there." In other words, what if your perception seems to be correct, and there may be a conflict here? Then you would move on to the next part of a Perception Check.

The second sub-step is to *ask what this additional set of facts means.* Following the same example, you would say something like, "Tell me how that came about." This response leaves room for a possible answer like this one: "We didn't mean to make the call without you, but we didn't expect the sudden change in the weather report and we couldn't reach you."

Again, you might not like the answer, but at least now you know what happened and why, so you allow for the possibility that it was nothing personal. Their response indicates there was no conspiracy against you, nor was there a deliberate attempt to undermine your power or authority on the production. The challenge is our emotions might trigger thoughts that are really judgments: they were wrong to do what they did; they don't care about my feelings; my vote doesn't count; and so on. This brings us to the third part of a Perception Check.

The third sub-step is to *turn judgment into curiosity.* This means stop evaluating, and instead gather more information. Avoid forming judgments that shut down receptiveness. Continuing with our example, you can engage your curiosity about the situation and ask something like, "When and where did you get the weather update?" With this response, you make room for the possibility of contradictory information sources, and you open up a dialogue about what actually happened, as opposed to your thoughts, judgments, or perception of what happened. You can discuss the real issue, which is how you came to not be involved in the decision-making about the set-up order.

The goal here is not to find fault or point fingers (who did what to whom and why); it's simply to account for the sequence of events. Contrast this response with a judgment that might sound like this: "Well, you should have waited to get hold of me before issuing the notice for change of set-up order!" Again, a response like this—effectively an accusation (i.e., "You failed to do something!")—would typically put the other person(s) into defensive mode, with all production team members involved careening towards a conflict.

You can always follow up with further data-gathering questions to get to the heart of the issue, such as, "How did you try to contact me about the changes, and when?" In this case, it may be the result of someone not wanting to call too late at night after wrapping, which is in fact an attitude of care and concern – far from a willful desire to exclude anyone. The result was still frustrating, but now the excluded party knows the real, and more benign, reason. The scenario could end with, "Thanks for the consideration, I appreciate it. I really don't mind getting a call on my cell phone late at night if it happens again." It's easy to get confrontational with someone who starts flinging accusations, but it's a lot harder to get mad at someone who's simply seeking to satisfy their curiosity.

To summarize, a Perception Check is always the first step towards conflict resolution. In the best-case scenario, when doing a Perception Check you may discover that there isn't actually a problem, and life goes on. In the worst-case scenario, you will get clarity on exactly what the issue is, so that you can work towards resolving what actually needs to be fixed, as opposed to what (or who) you imagine needs to be fixed.

If after doing a Perception Check you determine that there really is something that needs to be dealt with, you will then move to the second step, which is to Synchronize Intent and Impact.

Step Two: Synchronize Intent and Impact.

If after a Perception Check you determine that there really is an issue that needs to be addressed, the next step is to set your intention to maximize the positive impact that you seek. In other words, the second step after the Perception Check is to get clear on your reason(s) for having the conversation so that it has the desired effect—namely, to clear the air, resolve the issue, and move forward with the relationship intact. This is critical because you want to be able to start the conversation on a positive footing. You want to make sure that the other person knows why you are raising the subject—you don't want them to have to guess at anything, because they could guess incorrectly. If the intention behind the conversation isn't clear and positive, there's a good chance it will be poorly received; the impact will be negative. Transparency is key.

Setting a positive intention and desired impact is also crucial because it allows you to check in with yourself first and make sure you have the "right" motivations for having the conversation. Of course by "right" motivation we mean the desire to prevent or resolve conflict. It must never be about proving yourself right, making the other person wrong, and/or having the last word. No matter how badly you may be hurting, the goal should never be to make them feel the same pain about the situation. It may feel satisfying in the short term, but that kind of intention only results in prolonged or escalated conflict.

As with the Perception Check, we recommend writing down your purpose for having the conversation with the other person. Be honest. At the same time, make sure that you set an intention that is honorable, i.e. one that is ultimately about repairing or strengthening the relationship. You might truly feel the need to convince the other person of your point of view if you think you are misunderstood, but continuing to argue your case would only make matters worse. Here are some examples of setting positive intentions and their intended impacts:

• "My intention is to understand what is going on between us so that we can get along better." (Not, "My intention is to let her know that I am fed up about how things are going between us, and if it doesn't stop, I am out.")

• "My intention is to talk about how decisions are made so that I feel more comfortable." (Not, "My intention is to put my foot down about the decision-making process and insist that we have a democratic vote.")

• "My intention is to express how I feel about how the auditions for the secondary roles are going so that I can get it off my chest and feel heard." (Not, "My intention is to tell him that the auditions are wasting everybody's time and he needs to wake up and smell the coffee.")

To recap, the point of setting our intention is to get clear about what (not who) needs to be discussed, in order to make sure that the resulting impact will be a positive and productive one. It's worth reiterating that unless we clarify our intentions from the outset, people may (incorrectly) infer our intention based on how they are being impacted by what we are saying: If what we say lands in such a way that they feel bad, they may assume that our intention was to hurt them. Conversely, we tend to assume that what we say will be received in the spirit in which it is intended, which is not always the case. This is why it's always critical to synchronize the intent of the conversation with its desired impact, and why both need to be positive and constructive.

When it comes to conflict prevention and resolution, there is very little room for assumptions. Speculation only makes a situation more difficult in the end, especially if it's unwarranted. It is all too common for conflict to have its origins in the dynamics between intent and impact, because it is alarmingly easy to incorrectly attribute motivations or misread the purpose behind someone's words or actions. Flare-ups can occur just because one party inadvertently utters the wrong word, and the other party assumes it was deliberately chosen to wound. As soon as there has been a disconnect between intentions and the resulting impact, the miscommunication continues.

Once the Perception Check is done, you have verified that there is indeed a situation that needs to be addressed, and you have set your intention in a way that will create the positive impact you desire, it's time to start talking to the other person. You are now ready to move to the third step in conflict resolution, which is to engage in conversation using "I" Statements.

Step Three: Use "I" Statements

The "I" Statement is so called not because there is anything inherently selfish or self-centered about it, but because the speaker is talking from their own personal experience of the situation. It's a way to signal that the person is offering one subjective point of view only. "I" Statements are a way to ensure there is never any blame, motivation, or fault attributed to the other person during the conversation, even accidentally. That's because when a sentence contains (and especially begins with) the word "You," the listener assumes that what is about to follow is inevitably some sort of accusation or attribution, i.e., "You said this," or, "You did that." Such expectations invariably shut down the listening process and provoke defensiveness. On hearing the trigger word "You," the listener prepares to fend off an imminent attack and is less open to engaging in productive dialogue. Speaking in "I" Statements ensures that you refer only to yourself, your perceptions, your feelings, and your interpretations. It's a good way to demonstrate that you're taking responsibility for your own contributions to the situation.

The basic formula for an "I" Statement is as follows, and it is adaptable to any situation:

I am/feel _____ [*describe feeling*]

about/when _____ [*describe issue*], and

I would appreciate it if _____ [*invitation to discuss*].

Working with the clear intentions used in the examples above, let us now turn them into "I" Statements. If my intention is to understand what is going on between us so that we can get along better, I may start the conversation like this:

"I am <u>worried</u> [*describes feeling*] about <u>the tension I feel between us</u>

[*describes issue*], and I would appreciate it if <u>we could take an afternoon</u> <u>sometime this week to sit down and talk about things</u> [*invitation to discuss*]."

To choose another illustrative example, if my intention is to talk about how decisions are made so that I feel more comfortable, I may start the conversation thus:

"I feel <u>uncomfortable</u> [*describes feeling*] about <u>our decision-making process</u> [*describes issue*], and I would appreciate it if <u>we could put this topic on the</u> <u>agenda for our next production meeting</u> [*invitation to discuss*]."

Finally, if my intention is to express how I feel about how the secondary-role auditions are going, I could start the conversation this way:

"I feel <u>a need to talk</u> [*describes feeling*] about <u>how the auditions are going</u> [*describes issue*], and I would appreciate it if <u>we take the next few minutes and</u> <u>focus on this</u> [*invitation to discuss*]."

In this last case, "a need to talk" isn't technically a feeling; as you'll recall from our previous discussion of *blaming feelings*, it's more of a thought or a judgment. It does, however, point directly to a need, i.e., a need for connection, to be heard, for increased mutual understanding, etc., so we can let it pass in this instance.

Once you have opened with your "I" Statement, and the other person has agreed to continue the discussion (whether immediately or at a future time), then it's time to move to the fourth and final step, which is to follow the Fifth House Creative Conversations Model.

Step Four: Follow the 5-Step Fifth House Creative Conversations Model

Following all five steps of the Fifth House Creative Conversations Model will greatly increase your chances of ensuring that the conversation stays focused and productive and results in a positive outcome. Continue to apply the two Guiding Principles of Conflict Resolution throughout the discussion: Avoid the Conflict Escalation Triggers, and always use Active

Listening. Never rush through the phases of this model. Take your time—the end result will be worth it. Depending on the situation, you may find that all you need is twenty minutes, or you may need to have a number of different meetings to work through the phases. It all depends on the complexity of the conflict and people's willingness to come to a resolution.

Let's assume you have assessed the situation using the diagnostic tools discussed in Part One and are reasonably certain that this is a situation that doesn't require third-party assistance. Let's also assume you have done the following:

1. *Performed your Perception Check* to make sure that there is actually a difficult issue—a conflict—that needs to be addressed with another person or people;

2. *Synchronized your Intention and the desired Impact* to ensure that you are taking next steps for the benefit of all concerned and to genuinely improve the situation; and

3. *Used "I" Statements* to invite a productive discussion that will lead to resolution of the issue.

Having accomplished these, you are now ready for Step Four, i.e., to begin your 5-step Fifth House Creative Conversation.

Note: it is possible that at this stage you aren't sure whether or not to seek outside help. You know there is a problem and you've done the diagnostics, but you still aren't absolutely certain whether help is required, or perhaps you think you need some help but for some reason the assistance you seek isn't readily available. If either one of these conditions exists, you could still follow the Fifth House Creative Conversations Model, but build into the discussion your uncertainty about doing this on your own. Be up front with the other person about the fact that you'd like to try—or that you feel uneasy about—resolving the conflict without any third-party assistance. Be equally clear that if things don't go well for any reason, you would like to agree to stop and work together to find someone who can assist you in resolving the problem.

Either way, if you've arrived at this point in an actual situation, then you are getting into the heart of conflict resolution. Congratulations! The road ahead may still be bumpy, but regardless of the outcome it will help to remind yourself that what you are about to do—address a conflict with another person—is very courageous. You are being authentic and transparent, qualities that are key elements of leadership. You are doing the right thing.

It will also help to remind yourself of these key points:

- Do your best to stick to all the tips and tools you've learned, such as decoding feelings, needs, and strategies (refer back to Part Two, starting on page 55) and engaging consistently in Active Listening (starting on page 97).

- Doing your best does not mean you will be perfect. You might even have a spectacular screw-up. All is not lost; hey, stuff happens! If something does go wrong on your end, you can either just acknowledge the error to the other person and move on, or you can ask to put a hold on the conversation and come back to it later on when you've regrouped. Either option should work.

- Resolving a conflict does not mean that everything will necessarily be rosy between you or will go back to the way it was before the conflict arose. If the conflict is of relatively low intensity and stays out of the realm of the personal, it will be fairly easy and natural for everyone to just forget about it and get back to normal. However, in other situations the conflict may be more complex, with significant hurt, frustration, or disappointment in play. In such cases, remember that healing between people, and within yourself, does not mean that no damage was ever done. Just as physical injuries often leave scars, so can mental or emotional wounds. It doesn't mean that the incident never happened. It just means that anything you have experienced, individually or together, does not govern your relationship—you do. If you collectively decide to fix things between you so you can get on with the business of making movies, then it will be so. Just do your best, and if you need help, get it.

The Five Steps of a Fifth House Creative Conversations Model

We call this process a *Creative Conversation* because it allows the parties to a conflict the chances to build something fresh, new, and vital from something that might feel stale, old, or unhealthy. We hope that framing it in this way will encourage people to participate with positive attitudes and expectations. The alternative is to assume that any such conversation will be just another gripe session or the continuation of an endless argument, fraught with negativity, and to act accordingly.

We also named them Creative Conversations because, once completed, these dialogues allows you to finally get on with the business of being creative. Often the process liberates the participants' energies and allows them to channel it in more productive ways, rather than bottling things up out of fear and anxiety.

Throughout the Conversation you will be doing your best to use all of the tips and skills that you have learned so far. It is critical that you go through the steps in sequence and do your best not to deviate from them. Resist the temptation to follow wherever the conversation takes you, for three key reasons:

First, you are in a tenuous situation and want to ensure a positive outcome. This means you will have to actively shape the course of the conversation to achieve the desired result—leave nothing to chance. Even improvised movie scenes follow certain cinematic rules! In order to maximize your chances of success, strategy is required.

Second, if genuine understanding is to take place between the participants, you are going to have to work at it. Naturally, most people only feel ready to resolve conflict once they feel understood, but mutual understanding doesn't happen on its own. You are going to have to take the time and effort to genuinely comprehend each other, in order to resolve matters and move on. Each of the steps in this model is designed to build understanding between you. Each level of understanding is a prerequisite for the next, deeper level of understanding.

Third, if you don't follow the steps, you may still end up fixing things—but they may be the wrong things. It's normal for people with the best of intentions to want to proceed straight to solutions. But while solutions are clearly desirable, it's necessary to first make sure that they are aimed at resolving the real, underlying issues and not merely addressing the symptoms.

For example, it may seem obvious that the solution to miscommunication between the director and First AD is to write things down. But it could be that the underlying issue is that the Director accidentally offended the First AD by saying something that the latter perceived as sarcasm. Or maybe the First AD interpreted something in the director's tone as insulting or offensive. In situations like these, communicating in writing is unlikely to address the underlying issue and may, in fact, only make things worse. Texting, memos, and email are generally poor means of communication for expressing anything but a very limited menu of things like meeting agendas, because all nuance of tone and other nonverbal cues are absent. Written communications can feel cold and distant. You know from your own experience that it's far too easy to misinterpret what someone intended as humour for something more serious and straightforward, or vice versa. So in this example, the cure might be worse than the disease.

This is why it's essential to avoid skipping any steps of the Creative Conversation and going straight to solutions. It's natural to want to resolve issues and get back to normal as quickly as possible. These desires and intentions are good and honourable. However, navigating through conflict and emotions can be tricky, and moving too quickly from problem to solution is seldom a good idea. Taking your time and doing things right are more likely to put everyone in the best frame of mind to use

UNHELPFUL COMMUNICATION

Warning! The following are examples of unhelpful communication. They have no place in the business of listening and will only serve to derail your efforts at resolving conflict:

- Criticizing

- Sarcasm

- Name-calling

- Unsolicited advice

- Ordering

- Threatening

- Mind-reading

- Exaggeration

- Interrupting

- Minimizing

- Reassuring (can easily be interpreted as patronizing)

- "Technique-ing" without sincerity (i.e., using conflict

their extraordinary creativity to find robust solutions and resolve matters on a more durable basis. In the long run it will save you more time, effort, and money.

resolution knowledge as leverage or to gain moral high ground)

- Focusing only on facts and disregarding feelings involved, or vice versa

- Clichés, etc.

- Monopolizing the conversation

- Changing the topic

Avoid doing any or all of these at all costs!

The Fifth House Creative Conversations Model is a powerful collaborative discussion because it demonstrates to everyone concerned that their perspectives are being taken seriously, and that the participants are all important, not because of their role or position but because they are human beings. Initiating a collaborative discussion with someone you are in conflict with shows that you care about them, and the situation, and that your intention is to arrive at a resolution that works for everyone. This will be received as a signal of respect and will create a safe atmosphere in which to discuss difficult issues. If you want the other person to get on board and roll up their sleeves to resolve things together with you, this is how they must experience you. In adhering to the steps of this Model, it's likely that the relationships between those involved will emerge stronger and with greater mutual respect.

The Five Steps of the Fifth House Creative Conversations Model are as follows:

1. Tell each other your stories.
2. Identify what you want to resolve.
3. Develop options and potential solutions.
4. Articulate agreement and set follow-up meeting.
5. Hold follow-up meeting(s) to ensure everything is working.

Let's analyze each stage of the Model and its constituent parts. If you follow along, you will notice that we have given you some "to do" tips for each of the stages. Generally speaking, if you are using the skills and applying the Guiding Principles while following each of these five steps, you will be conducting a bona fide conflict resolution session. Readers of *Keep the Drama in Front of the Camera!* (and our previous book, *Conflict Resolution for Musicians*) have exclusive access to an annotated example of a Fifth House Creative Conversations dialogue illustrating each of the stages of the model. Visit www.fifthhousegroup.com/bookbonus to download the companion document that steps through a Creative Conversation using a fictionalized entertainment industry example drawn from real life.

Step 1. Tell each other your stories.

1a. Describe the problem or situation you have come to talk about. The primary thing to remember here is that you stay very far away from using the Conflict Escalation Triggers as described on page 84. Use neutral, non-accusatory words and tone. Avoid blame or judgments. Never exaggerate. The best way is to start with an "I" Statement (e.g., "I felt _____ when I noticed that _____ was happening, and my goal in having this meeting is to _____" as per the three-part "I" Statement model recommended on page 119).

1b. *Invite the other person to speak about the problem or situation from their perspective.* Listen to understand by using Active Listening skills (see page 97) and by staying genuinely curious about the other person's perspective.

1c. *When the other person has finished describing the situation from their perspective, and you have demonstrated that you have understood what they have said* (see page 105), it is then *your turn to describe the situation from your perspective.* It is tough to do, but make it your goal to understand the other person first, *before* you try to get them to understand you. Quite simply, if they feel heard, understood, and taken seriously, they are far more likely to be willing and able to make the effort to hear, understand, and take you seriously. In other words, do for them first, what you would like them to do for you.

2. Identify what you want to resolve.

2a. *Have an honest and open discussion about what is important to each of you.* Take as much time as you need, because everything else from here on out hinges on this. Put everything on the table: concerns, hopes, expectations, values and priorities – it's all valid and useful. When the time comes to find solutions, you will want to make sure you are fixing the right things, and you can only do that if you get this part right. As always, stay focused on what needs to be fixed, not who. Avoid taking a position or going straight to solutions; you'll develop solutions collaboratively, in due course. Talk about what your interests are; as everyone is doing so, gently help each other to articulate what might be underlying those concerns (without putting words in their mouths, of course). Support them. Explore the needs that are at stake for each of you. Get clear about what the real crux of the problem is all about, for each participant. Write these things down. Again, take as much time as you need. Don't rush it—get it right.

2b. *Make a list of the things that need to be fixed and/or issues that need to be resolved.* From all of the above (in Step 2a), make a list of the issues that each of you have identified as being important. They may be different, and they may be the same for each of you. If there are multiple issues, agree on a starting point and the order or sequence for addressing each of them in turn. There is no "right" or "wrong" order; you might want to tackle the most contentious issue(s) first, or, conversely, build up to that point with the smaller, less contentious issue(s) in order to gain momentum and goodwill. Consider sandwiching the tougher issues in the middle, so you gain valuable traction early in the conversation, and reward yourselves by winding down with the less risky issues at the end.

2c. *Ask if there is anything else that is important to him or her that they might want to share.* Check to make sure nothing has been left unsaid. It is possible that someone may still have something to express that, for whatever reason, they haven't felt comfortable bringing up yet. If there is something else that comes up, repeat (2a) and (2b) above.

3. Develop options and potential solutions.

3a. *Together, brainstorm creative ways of resolving the issues and taking care of what is important to you.* We call these options because they're all possible solutions, or parts of the solution, to the problem at hand. They should remain potential solutions for most of this stage; avoid the temptation to leap straight to declaring the most obvious, quickest, or easiest answer. Let all the ideas marinate.

It's best to do the brainstorming while sitting side-by-side and recording ideas on paper or on a white board, flip chart, or other medium. This symbolically demonstrates a joint effort in solving the problem and reinforces the idea at a subtle psychological level. Talking across a table places a physical and psychological barrier between you and puts you in literal opposition to each other.

As you proceed, follow these key brainstorming principles:

- *Quantity is more important than the quality*, at least initially. The greater the sheer number of ideas you have to work with, the more creative you can get with your possible solutions. Few, if any, will be perfect, but don't dismiss them out of hand. You will go back later and either develop or filter out the less viable ones. The more ideas you have to work with, the better.

- *All ideas or fragments of ideas, however tentative, should be recorded without judgment.* Avoid commenting on any of the ideas or committing to any particular idea or proposed solution until all parties have had their say and the brainstorming is truly exhausted. This means no censoring or shooting down the other's ideas, and no self-censoring, either.

The goal of this step is to remain open to all creative input, no matter how outlandish or unworkable the ideas may seem at first. Effective brainstorming encourages the rapid, open flow of creativity, and it lessens the likelihood that someone's feelings will be hurt by editorializing on those ideas as they emerge; needless to say, this will only fuel the conflict. Besides, you never know which idea will provide the platform for the best, most durable solution, or who will contribute it. The more all parties can contribute to the solution(s), the more likely everyone will be able to throw their wholehearted support behind it/them.

3b. *Identify the potential solution(s) by agreeing on the most promising ideas and developing them further.* The ideal solution seldom exists "in the wild" and usually needs some modification to make it more viable or appealing to one or more of the parties. An idea may be unworkable in its present form, but, with a little tweaking, an otherwise unlikely solution may come to life. Make use of blue-sky questions like "What if…?" and "Why not…?"

For example, let's say the pre-production team is brainstorming ways to produce a particular special visual effect, but there are serious disagreements about how to achieve it. One possible answer might be to combine the competing ideas and make it part practical effect, part computer-generated imaging (CGI), instead of all one or the other. If time is the consideration, ask how you might overcome the time issue even if you can't extend the production deadline. What if you could shorten the production cycle by bringing in more computing power and visual FX artists? What if you could recycle footage that already exists elsewhere? What would you do if time or money were no object? If budget is the main stumbling block, ask how money might be liberated from elsewhere in the budget, or crowdfunded. Or maybe the effect doesn't need to be seen at all, but just implied? (In *Aliens*, the creature was all the more frightening because the audience seldom saw it in full physical incarnation until near the end.) These blue-sky thought experiments may not produce the ideal solution, but they could. They'll certainly open up the avenues for creativity and they just might bring more harmony and cohesiveness to a team working hard to find a mutually satisfactory solution.

Eventually identifying the "right" or "best" solution can be a challenge, and in this example the standard for "best" solution is fairly obvious – it needs to work within the available budget and time frame and be feasible for the production team to execute. It's not always so obvious how to satisfy the parties when the conflict is more complex or the issues are highly emotional. Still, there is a way to ensure that the solution chosen is at least fair to all parties—and not just "fair" to one party because it works out better for them. If the decision reached is not perceived as fair and acceptable to all, it won't be a durable one. Conflict will continue to simmer. The goal is to establish similarly objective criteria for choosing the optimal solution.

To take a simple example, if you were negotiating the asking price of a second-hand RED digital camera, you could use the average Craigslist or eBay asking price for the same make, year, and model as one criterion for determining what is fair to both the buyer and the seller. (A well-known psychological phenomenon predicts that people are likely to value their own asset higher, simply because it belongs to them.) Neither party involved in the negotiation determined that average price; the market (more specifically, other buyers and sellers on Craigslist or eBay) did. In that sense it's a neutral, objective standard. Otherwise, setting an arbitrary value – say, pricing it at ten percent below the price of a brand new model – risks favouring one party over the other, and by definition the solution will not be fair to both parties. Remember, too, that the best solution may in fact be a combination of ideas, either in their original form or in some modified version.

But what if you have a conflict over treatment of another human being?

What if the conflict is over a process-oriented issue, such as decision-making or hiring practices? Objective standards like market rates or list prices and so forth aren't as obvious in cases where you need to consider people's feelings and other complicating factors, but they're available. You might, for example, use past precedent as one standard of fair treatment. In other words, how were similar situations handled previously? Unless the precedents themselves were found to be inherently unfair or undesirable, it would make sense not to depart to radically from those standards in your current situation.

If the present circumstances are sufficiently serious, another fair, objective standard could be the prior outcomes of court cases or human rights tribunals. Even if your particular conflict hasn't advanced quite to that stage, these solutions could be helpful yardsticks against which to measure the fairness of the ideas generated in your problem-solving phase. Again, the idea remains the same: to find some means of testing the proposed solutions against some independent standard.

Only once the brainstorming is truly finished and all ideas are completely exhausted, is it time to go through each and every solution listed and weigh them against each person's interests, needs, and any objective decision-making criteria you have set. (One more free tool you can use for this purpose is the Decision Matrix, available for download from our web site under the Resources section.) Avoid rushing to judgment at all costs. Brainstorming is a wonderful opportunity to use your creativity.

4. Articulate Agreement and set follow-up meeting.

4a. *Agree on the most appropriate solution(s).* The "most appropriate" solutions are those that realistically address the greatest number of concerns and needs of all parties and achieve a truly fair, "win-win" outcome as described in Step 3b above. If you've followed all the steps to this point and have had a sufficiently productive, open-minded brainstorming session, then chances are you'll have no trouble identifying the most workable resolution.

4b. *Clearly articulate the terms of the agreement.* Identify and record, for example, who does what, when, where, and how. Be very specific and ensure that all are clear on their respective roles and responsibilities – you confirm yours, and everyone else is equally clear on theirs. Nothing will undo a satisfying agreement (and lead right back into conflict) more predictably than having someone fail to uphold their end of the deal, and one way to ensure they keep their word is to simply make sure they know what's expected of them. Clarity precedes accountability. Never assume everyone automatically understands or remembers what's been agreed upon.

4c. *Develop a contingency plan to address what you will do if things don't go as planned.* While this collaborative discussion model is relatively foolproof, things can sometimes go sideways. It's always a good idea to have a "Plan B," even at the best of times, so you can have one to fall back on in the event your original win-win solution doesn't stand the test of time. This contingency plan could involve bringing in outside help, stepping through the Creative Conversation model a second time, invoking a higher authority (say, the Producer or some other designated individual), or a combination of things – whatever you collectively agree will be an effective backstop to prevent things from going completely pear-shaped.

4d. *Revisit confidentiality to be clear on what can and cannot be shared with others.* You might, for example, decide that it's OK for everyone to share with their significant others how the experience impacted them emotionally, but it's not OK to share who said or did what. Conversely, you might collectively decide that nothing about the situation should ever be discussed outside the studio/boardroom/set or wherever you are. Whatever provides the most peace of mind and feeling of safety/security for all parties is the right approach.

4e. *Write all of this (sub-steps A to D) down!* All parties should keep a copy of what has been decided and recorded. This is a simple way of preventing any potential problems because someone has forgotten exactly what was agreed upon, details were overlooked or mixed up, or any other reason; you can always refer back to the written notes as needed. In fact, it's a good idea to make a habit of periodically checking in to see how you are doing with the agreement, even if things seem to be going well. If someone is starting to feel things slip, then it's a good opportunity to reaffirm the agreement and recommit to upholding it. If everything is indeed fine, then you can feel positive about the strength and solidity of your agreement.

4f. *Close the conversation.* Thank the other party for agreeing to work with you to resolve the situation. This brings a sense of closure to the incident and rewards everyone for their patience and hard work.

4g. *Set a date and time for a follow-up meeting.* This is critical. The reasons for this are explained in Step 5, below.

4h. *Give yourselves a huge pat on the back!* You've earned it.

5. Hold a follow-up meeting to ensure everything is working.

It's dangerous to assume that everything will go as planned, especially once the talking is over and the hard work is done. People are people; they fall back into familiar, comfortable routines; things get forgotten; and before long there's another upset. If you follow up diligently to make sure everyone stays on track, in one or a series of meetings, there's a greater likelihood that any decisions made during the problem-solving Creative Conversation will stick. Revisit the agreement(s) periodically to make sure it's still working. There's no requirement that a solution that isn't working to everyone's benefit can't be changed.

Perhaps most importantly, make sure that everyone looks out for each other. It's easy (and natural) for everyone to take care to protect their own feelings and needs, but it can't come at the expense of someone else's.

Back to Ones: Summary

In this section we identified and learned to apply two Guiding Principles of conflict prevention and resolution: avoiding the common conflict escalation triggers and using Active Listening techniques. Triggers include using the word "You" in any conversation related to a conflict, because the other party will inevitably mistake it for an accusation or attack of some sort. Often the words that follow "You" attribute someone's behaviour to bad intent, carelessness, or some other cause that is likely to be as incorrect as it is dishonourable, and thus begins a cycle of blame and retribution. Other triggers include dredging up old, irrelevant issues or attempting to "triangulate" by winning others over to your side, usually by telling tales that cast you as the victim or hero and the other party as the bad guy of the story.

Another way to ensure your conflict resolution conversations don't go off-track is to use a checklist to ensure you follow all four steps to conflict resolution, beginning with a Perception Check; synchronizing the intent and the impact of the conversation; using "I" Statements; and following the 5-step Fifth House Creative Conversations Model. The first of these steps is simply a way to verify whether there's actually a problem to begin with, or if it's just someone's perception that is the apparent issue. A Perception Check can often eliminate the need for any subsequent work by ruling out a genuine problem and clearing up a mistaken impression. If it doesn't, the second step is a way to ensure that any negative impact of the conversation and its content—which might cause pain or discomfort for one or more of the people involved—is clearly unintentional. The real purpose of the conversation (and this second step) is not to make anyone feel bad or wrong, but to ensure the intentions behind the parties' words and deeds (which are generally good and noble) have the desired emotional effect (which can otherwise turn out negative and hurtful).

Once this foundation is established, keep the lines of communication open by ensuring you speak only from your own feelings and experience, thus precluding the possibility that you might accidentally blame or accuse the other person by using the trigger word, "You." Along with speaking from your own feelings and experience in "I" Statements, use Active Listening, which includes paraphrasing, summarizing, and practicing empathy. Being careful not to interrupt, periodically restate and reframe the other's words to give them the opportunity to correct any mistaken impressions and to reassure them they've truly been heard. Finally, following each of the five steps in the Fifth House Creative Conversations Model (especially if you prepare well using the checklists and worksheets provided) will help ensure a positive outcome for all involved.

Close-up: Special Issues in Film & TV

In our entertainment industry consulting work, questions about how to handle specific situations that arise in the workplace almost invariably involve three things that are especially applicable to the film and TV industry: dealing with conflicts involving unions and guilds; time pressure; and situations involving hierarchical relationships. It's worth a special detour to examine them here.

It should be noted that if you are involved in any of these scenarios, you might need to consider them a little more carefully to determine whether or not it is appropriate for you to tackle them on your own. Due to their inherently challenging dynamics, they may require a skill level that is more typically found at the professional conflict resolution practitioner level.

Nevertheless, the following are some tips to help your overall management of these situations.

Unions, Guilds, and Advocacy Involvement

We know that issues involving the many film and TV unions and guilds can be quite contentious from time to time. Attempts at conflict resolution in these cases are often best handled by a mediator, unless the parties are at the very beginning stages of discussing matters, eager to work things out to everyone's mutual satisfaction, and determined to prevent escalation. If the latter, favourable conditions prevail in your situation, here are some recommendations to help facilitate discussions:

- *Keep the conversation focused on the issue.* Go back to our escalation model (page 91) and review the triggers. If you are able to discuss the matter without going into "You" mode (unless of course it's to deliver a compliment!), then you will be able to stay focused on the issue at hand. If the other people in the discussion stray into "You" mode, remember to avoid taking the bait. Simply don't respond, and instead guide them back to the issue. This is one of your most powerful techniques for making sure the conversation doesn't get derailed and stays productive.

- *Treat any union/guild reps, or anyone else in an advocacy or supportive role who might be involved in the discussion, as a valued team member.* They are part of the problem-solving effort to find a solution to whatever needs to be addressed. Yes, they may sometimes be positional or come across as aggressive. It is tempting sometimes to treat people in these roles as a disruptive force or even as an opponent. However, they are there to do a job and to fulfill a valuable function. When it's our turn and we need union representation or advocacy, it sure feels good to have them there, so their role needs to be acknowledged and honoured as vital. Thus, treating them as a team member will go a long way towards keeping the discussion respectful. Remember too that union reps can be very helpful when it comes to reality-checking. Sometimes the problem-solving participants may have an idea or solution that really isn't practical or realistic, or may not be part of known standards of practice, and

134

in these cases union reps will be able to identify these potential roadblocks. They can also work with their member/client(s) to propose more realistic options.

- *Make sure that anything important or agreed to is recorded, in writing.* If the situation allows for it, write key points on a flipchart or white board as they are identified or as agreements are reached. This allows everyone to see them at the same time and confirm their agreement with the content on the spot. This technique will keep the conversations immediate instead of having to go back to them later. Have participants take pictures of the flipchart/white board notes with their phones, so that they have an instant record of what was written down and agreed upon. If it is not possible to use flipcharts, then have someone record everything in writing, reading it out loud as you go along. Afterwards, these notes can be typed up as minutes and emailed out to everyone concerned.

Time Sensitivity

The film industry can be a brutally fast-paced environment. Extreme time crunches are a daily occurrence; even the best-planned productions are always fighting the clock. There may be very little available space to breathe, never mind sit down and work through a conflict properly, step by step. As such, fast reactions and immediate decisions without regard to individual feelings are par for the course. Naturally this is a perfect breeding ground for disputes to arise, as we've often heard from clients and friends in the business. The relentless time pressure works against a fundamental human need – the need to be heard and understood. If you find yourself in a situation where there is very little time to discuss, yet the outcome is critical for you, here are some tips to help manage that type of interaction:

- *As with union and advocacy involvement discussed above, keep things focused on the issue.* Go back to our escalation model (page 91) and review the triggers. If you are able to discuss the matter without going into "You" mode (unless of course it is to deliver a compliment), then you will be able to stay focused on the issue at hand. If the other people in the discussion stray into "You" mode, remember not to take the bait. Simply don't respond, and instead guide them back to the issue. This is one of your most powerful techniques for making sure the conversation doesn't derail and stays productive.

- *When the conversation begins, the very first time you hear someone express a feeling, use empathy.* Acknowledge and validate the emotions; it's how they're experiencing things. As the conversation evolves and participants continue to express their feelings, keep responding with empathy. Yes, time is pressing, some folks will just want to press on, with little patience for any touchy-feely stuff. There is, however, real truth in the expression that sometimes you need to "slow down in order to speed up." A strategic approach will ensure that the conversation has a positive outcome, one that is robust and durable. Therefore, invest the extra time required to show empathy to the person who is expressing their emotions. A few seconds or minutes can save considerable time and energy in the long run. You don't have to agree, you don't even have to care – but you do need to get them feeling heard and understood if you want them to be less positional and defensive. Less positional and defensive means that the conversation is going to go better. We often underestimate how profoundly simple yet powerful empathy is. It is one of the fastest ways to break down the barriers between people and one of the quickest ways to build trust and respect. Spend the extra little bit of time in ensuring that people feel heard and understood, and you will likely be pleased with your return on that investment. Go back to page 109 and review empathy as you prepare for your conversation.

- *Remember that haste makes waste.* Things that are done quickly are often done without due care and attention. The same is true with decisions. People may not have heard things properly, or some may not have interpreted what was said the same way as others have. They may misremember or flat out forget because their brains are so full and they have a hundred pressing things at the same time. Any or all of these can result in further conflict, simply because participants then leave the conversation thinking things are resolved, only to later find that all parties were not all on the same page. Make it easy for everyone. As a decision is made, repeat it out loud to confirm everyone's agreement, and then text or message it out to everyone involved, on the spot. Do it right the first time and you'll save time in the long run.

Hierarchy and Power Imbalances

Situations where there are power or hierarchical imbalances – such as in the film and TV industry, where there is a very clear pecking order on any set – can be rather uncomfortable. Having to go through a difficult conversation with someone who is higher up the ladder than you are, or who holds the purse strings, or any number of different ways in which one person has influence over another, is often quite challenging. If your relationship with this person is generally pretty good, and you aren't too concerned about being able to speak openly and honestly with them, then the following tips will help you along the way. See our Conflict Assessment Chart in the Appendix as a guide to assist you in this decision.

However, if you are in any way afraid of this person, or you have serious concerns that talking with them on your own might negatively impact you, your reputation, or your career, then it may be best to connect with a professional conflict resolution practitioner first. This person could help you assess whether or not going it alone is the appropriate choice, and/or could also give you some coaching in order to better prepare you to have that conversation. You can consult our website in order to access these services and other resources, at www.fithhousegroup.com, and look for the Resources page. With those caveats in mind, the following are some tips to assist you in having the conversation where power dynamics are at play:

- *Book a time and place to meet that works to your advantage.* If you are a morning person, schedule your discussion in the morning, and not at the end of the day when you are likely to be already drained of energy. If you're a night owl, go for something in the evening, not in the morning when your head is still clearing. Choose a day that you know won't be too crowded with other things, when you won't be preoccupied with a looming deadline or that sort of thing. Choose a location that you feel the most comfortable in. The boss's office may not be the best idea. If you are more relaxed in a coffee shop setting, or a pub, then go for that. In other words, make the time of day, the day itself, and the location, something that works best for you. This will give you more of a psychological lift in the discussion.

- *Prepare well for your conversation.* As much as possible, do what you can to minimize the stress of the conversation. Stressors include being unsure of what to say, how to say it, or when to say it. If you are already feeling somewhat intimated by the nature of the power imbalance between the two of you, then it is important to feel ready and strong when you do start to talk. Preparation will go a long way towards this. Setting yourself up for success in this case means creating a conducive internal environment (i.e., your emotional well-being). This means you aren't wondering, questioning, and second-guessing, but instead you are clear, focused, and have a plan. The five steps of the Fifth House Creative Conversations Model, beginning on page 122, will support you with the latter. You may also want to consider preparing with a friend, trusted colleague, or anyone else who you know will play a practical, helpful, and morally supportive role.

- *Be honest.* If you are worried about opening up to this person, with the result having a potential negative impact on your finances, career, project, or other aspect of your life, tell them so. Being careful to own your fear and not have it emerge as an accusation (using "I" Statements!), let them know at the beginning of the conversation. Your honesty will set the tone for what follows. At the very least, by putting it on the table, you won't be distracted by trying to hide your concerns or by trying to maneuver cleverly around the reality of the situation. There's a certain relief in expressing yourself. It is also possible that you will be pleasantly surprised by how the other person responds to your openness. Most decent folks respond well to someone that they can tell is being genuine. If you've assessed that it's OK for you to have this conversation on your own with the individual in question, despite existing or perceived power imbalances, and if you're practicing the three tips in this section, then all that's left is to give your partner in conversation the benefit of the doubt and to go ahead and start talking from the heart.

Plot Twist: Differences in Jurisdiction

In this era of globalization, and thanks to relevant treaties and opportunities for funding support, the business is seeing a significant increase in international co-productions. So-called "runaway" productions are also taking advantage of lower exchange rates in foreign territories and/or competing regional tax credits. From a conflict perspective, this means taking into account the important differences in how jurisdictions influence the way conflicts can or should be resolved.

For example, in most states in the U.S. (and a few other countries), labour law recognizes something called "at-will employment." This is a legal/contractual concept wherein employees can be dismissed by an employer at any time, for any reason, without first having to establish "just cause" for termination. (The flip side of this is that employees can voluntarily leave for any reason, or no reason at all, at any time, without providing advance notice.) Needless to say, this rule makes it tempting to simply fire a subordinate rather than make the effort to work out differences between the parties.

This notion of "at-will" employment is in direct contrast to the majority of countries that currently have very different employment regimes. Canada in particular has a long tradition of strict human rights protection, which makes it far more difficult to fire an employee legally, even with cause. This is critical to remember for U.S. employers. At the time of writing, Toronto and Vancouver rank third and fourth, respectively, right behind L.A. and New York, as the major centers of production in North America, and both cities are enjoying increased cross-border production activity. Although the exact steps may vary from one Canadian region to another (because business is mostly regulated at the provincial level), there is generally a sort of "three-strikes" rule that requires employers to carefully document a progressive series of disciplinary actions prior to terminating an employee for cause.

A complete discussion of this process is beyond the scope of this book, but suffice it to say that *it's generally much easier, cheaper, and in everyone's best interests in both the short and long run to resolve conflicts through the tools and techniques described here*, rather than act in haste and repent at leisure. Even in the U.S., where "at-will employment" is predominant, a lot of expensive and enervating litigation can be avoided by resolving differences in a more collaborative, and less combative, fashion.

Denouement: The "Nuclear Option"

"Okay," you may say. "What if I try all of this and it still doesn't work? What then?"

Let's be clear: even the most dedicated student of conflict resolution will find on occasion that practicing all of the tools and techniques learned in this book will not guarantee a mutually satisfactory outcome. It sometimes happens that you may reach a bona fide impasse, even when working with a conflict resolution professional such as a mediator, facilitator, or conflict coach. After all, it takes two to tango, and eventually you may encounter a person for whom a scorched-earth, win-lose policy is preferable to a win-win outcome. Where genuine mental health issues are concerned (for example, dealing with someone suffering from narcissistic personality disorder), the tools and techniques learned here may have limited effectiveness, and may not be appropriate without some other intervention. Sometimes the relationship has already deteriorated to a point that is beyond salvage.

That's when you may decide to exercise what we call the "nuclear option," which is simply to walk away from the situation and the relationship. We hope this won't be the case, but we'd be remiss in not being forthright and realistic about this possibility. We also caution against invoking the "nuclear option" too soon or too readily, because most situations aren't truly past the point of no return until and unless all of conflict resolution skills you've just learned have been applied consistently, faithfully, and still no progress has been made whatsoever.

If this sounds depressing, take heart. Even though there may be times when we are unable to achieve agreement, we can always achieve greater mutual understanding. And the beauty of conflict resolution is that mutual understanding means a healthier environment for all concerned, even if we can't always have our way.

That's a Wrap: Conclusion

By now you have probably learned far more than you ever thought you would learn—or might want to learn—about resolving conflicts successfully. You might have approached this book (or at least the topic of conflict) full of dread. Our hope is that if we define conflict as merely a signal that something, somewhere, needs to change, it gives cause for optimism in the sense that you can empower yourself with the tools to make the necessary adjustments.

We began by taking a brief, high-level look at the history of conflict in the film and television industry, which is long, dramatic, and has left a trail of economic and artistic destruction. It's sad to think of the great works never made or negatively affected, and the careers effectively ruined, all because of needless, preventable (or at least manageable) conflicts. Think of how much creative output and how many careers could have been salvaged if these conflicts had only been managed well instead. There is no doubt that conflict can be expensive, given the number of high-profile cases that have ended in litigation or the departure of marquee talent from a big-budget production. But much of its cost can remain invisible to the naked eye, manifesting in a wide array of problems, from absenteeism to stress and physical illness, and ending in significant financial loss resulting from production delays or replacing key personnel in mid-shoot.

The good news is that you are now armed with some basic conflict theory (from Parts One and Two) to help you better understand how conflicts start and why they can so quickly and easily spiral out of control. You now know, for example, the difference between mere disagreement, conflict, and harassment or bullying, and that sometimes conflict can actually be productive and healthy if handled well. If handled poorly, the distinctions are important because each requires its own skill set to manage effectively, and each lets you know that things have progressed to an undesirable stage. You also know how to recognize the four warning signs of conflict (emotional, physical, behavioural, and relational) so that you can stop a conflict in its tracks before it has a chance to devolve into a worse situation.

Having read this far, you have gained sufficient knowledge to not only assess a conflict situation on the basis of emotions, trust, history, and power dynamics, but also to determine when it's time to get help managing or resolving a conflict. There are several types of conflict resolution assistance available, and you can decide the most appropriate to a particular level of conflict and where to locate resources for any help you might need. Even if you still don't feel confident in your own conflict resolution abilities, you can relax in the knowledge that some form of expert help is at hand regardless of your current skill level.

Along the way you have analyzed the inner mechanics of conflict and examined the critical role that feelings play in conflict situations. You have learned how to interpret feelings that may arise in conflict situations, or at least developed the necessary curiosity to help you diagnose the situation. You can use the information to help identify your own needs and better understand the needs of the other party—even if they're having trouble naming and understanding their own feelings.

Needs, whether or not we recognize them (or even fully comprehend them), are central to conflict resolution. You have learned that if another cast or crew member craves acknowledgement for their contributions (to cite one example), you have an opportunity to meet those needs without necessarily having to sacrifice your own. All you have to do is remember to occasionally offer genuine praise, even if you don't keep a particular take or shot. If they have a more process-oriented need, like the need to have their voice heard in a discussion or decision, then you can make a point of inviting and acknowledging their input. Neither means you'll necessarily agree, just that you'll find it easier to move on without worrying whether conflict will erupt, because you will have met an important need – one that, for any number of reasons, people often find difficult to express in words.

In the context of conflict situations and human behaviour, the term strategy was defined as an attempt to meet those needs, however clumsy or unintentionally hurtful the strategy may be. We resort to these reactionary, primitive strategies when we haven't got the words or tools to express our needs more effectively—often because we're in the midst of an emotional storm. The ability to recognize and interpret strategies allows you look past the turmoil and get beneath the otherwise confusing or frustrating behaviours to figure out what's really going on. You might need to say or do something – or avoid saying or doing something – in order to meet the other person's needs and thus prevent or de-escalate a conflict.

Another skill you learned in Part Two is how to differentiate authentic feelings from blaming feelings. This, too, is critical, because when someone's ability to articulate their feelings drops (including our own), you can now do two things: first, you can prevent yourself from being triggered by someone else's blaming-feeling statements, and, second, you can interpret the situation correctly and avoid fanning the flames.

In Part Three you delved deeper into essential conflict prevention and resolution skills, including the application of two Guiding Principles: avoiding the common Conflict Escalation Triggers and using Active Listening techniques. From there, it's a relatively straightforward process to follow a checklist to ensure you walk through all four steps to conflict resolution. These four steps, which are broken into their constituent parts, begin with conducting a Perception Check. This is followed by synchronizing your Intent and desired Impact to ensure a positive outcome; speaking only in "I" Statements; and following the Fifth House Creative Conversations Model, as outlined here.

Congratulations! We hope you've been able to follow along and perhaps even apply some of your newly acquired skills to a situation you might be facing right now in your production team, organization, or even your personal life. In getting this far you have joined a select (but, fortunately, growing) community of immensely talented, creative people who have the necessary skills, attitudes, and knowledge to prevent conflicts from occurring in the first place. If conflicts do occur, which is almost inevitable given the amazing diversity of people and personalities on this beautiful planet, your expertise will reduce the likelihood of their escalating out of control. You are now far better equipped to help resolve them effectively. Practice your conflict resolution skills, because, like anything else worth learning, they require patience and commitment to develop. We wish you every success in your career, and may you spread joy and harmony everywhere you go, not only with your film or TV career but with your life skills, too.

Cut! And print.

AFTERWORD

Thank you for reading *Keep the Drama in Front of the Camera!* If you haven't already, we invite you to join the conversation by Liking our Facebook pages:

www.facebook.com/KeepTheDramaInFrontOfTheCamera and www.facebook.com/FifthHouseGroup

We would be grateful if you would post a review on sites like Goodreads.com, your favorite online retailer, or wherever you discover, read, and discuss books or other topics of interest to film and television industry people. Please remember to support your local bookseller, too.

We'd love to hear from you! Email us at connect@fifthhousegroup.com.

Namaste,

Ken & Helene.

ABOUT THE AUTHORS

Fifth House Group President **Ken Ashdown** is a lapsed musician and former music journalist, indie label entrepreneur, and major label executive. Over his career Ken has worked with some of the music industry's biggest stars, including Shania Twain, Def Leppard, Bon Jovi, John Mellencamp, Dire Straits, New Order, David Bowie, the Pixies, and U2. He served as Vice President at PolyGram Group Canada (Mercury/Polydor division) and later at QDesign Corporation, subsequently purchased by Digital Theatre Systems. An award-winning, certified adult educator, Ken spent several years as Head of Department at Vancouver Film School's ground-breaking Entertainment Business Management transmedia program and has been hailed as a "master teacher," serving as a special consultant on dozens of films. He earned his Master of Arts (MA) degree in Music Business Management (with Distinction) from the University of Westminster in London, England, and is a Belbin® Team Role Accredited facilitator. Among other associations, he is a proud member of the Cultural Human Resources Council and the Music and Entertainment Industry Educators Association.

Helene Arts, CEO of Fifth House Group, started off thinking that she was going to become a lawyer, but by 1995 she realized that the gods had other plans for her, and thus began her career as a professional mediator. Since then she has been a full-time consultant in the field of conflict resolution within criminal, family, and civil court systems, and in not-for-profit and corporate workplace settings. Along the way she became fascinated with group dynamics, and in 2004 completed a Masters in Human Systems Intervention at Concordia University in Montreal, Quebec, becoming a specialist in group intervention. For over ten years Helene has also taught university courses in subjects such as mediation, inter-personal communication, group dynamics, conflict resolution, organizational conflict, and group facilitation. She holds a special place in her heart for creative people of all kinds.

APPENDIX:
WORKSHEETS AND CHECKLISTS

The worksheets in this section are meant to help you prepare for handling a difficult situation on your own. There are four in all:

1.   *Conflict Assessment Worksheet* (to help evaluate the emotions, trust, history, and power dynamic in a conflict)

2.   *Conflict Assistance Chart* (to help you determine what kind of assistance, if any, is most appropriate for your situation)

3.   *Preparation Checklist* (to help ensure you are ready to engage in healthy, productive dialogue towards conflict resolution)

4.   *Fifth House Creative Conversations Preparation Worksheet* (to help you prepare for the 5-step Fifth House Creative Conversation to follow).

You can also download and print PDF versions from the Fifth House Group website (www.fifthhousegroup.com/resources) any time you find yourself needing to prepare for a potentially challenging or uncomfortable conversation; where applicable, completed examples are also available to show you how to make best use of them.

Before attempting to resolve a conflict on your own, make sure you can put a check mark in every box on the Preparation Checklist! When things get emotional, it's far too easy to accidentally say or do something that winds up causing further distress unless you've really done your best to have a genuinely collaborative problem-solving discussion. Use the many other resources at your disposal on the Fifth House Group website, and good luck!

Conflict Assessment Worksheet

Criteria	Score				
Emotions (1 = Low levels of emotion; 5 = intense or high levels)	1	2	3	4	5
Trust (1 = Good, strong trust between people; 5 = Poor or no trust)	1	2	3	4	5
History (1 = Little or no history of conflict; 5 = long or substantial history of conflict)	1	2	3	4	5
Power (1 = Equality of power/fair & balanced; 5 = great imbalance/high inequality)	1	2	3	4	5
Total score:					
Interpretation: A score of **4-6** indicates you can probably safely handle this situation on your own; **7-13** indicates you should probably seek some third-party assistance; **14-20** indicates you should probably not attempt to resolve the conflict without some professional intervention.					
Notes, observations, and conclusion:					

Conflict Assistance Chart

Note: Use the previous *Conflict Assessment Worksheet* first to evaluate the relative levels of emotion, trust, history, and any power imbalance in the conflict. Then use the *Conflict Assistance Chart* to determine the most appropriate form(s) of assistance in your situation, based on your assessment.

Factor:	Coaching	Negotiation	Facilitation	Mediation
Emotions	Any	Low to Medium	Medium	High
Trust Levels	Any	Good to Medium	Medium	Low
History	Any	None or Positive	Some	Some or Negative
Power Imbalance	Any	None or Some	Some	Yes

Preparation Checklist

Preparation Checklist	
Item	**Check ✓**
Description of conflict: *I have assessed and described the conflict in terms of the Emotions, Trust, History, and Power dynamic, and it is appropriate for us to handle this without a third party.*	
Triggers to watch out for: *I have learned the common Conflict Escalation Triggers and avoided using them. I have noticed when others use them and avoided getting triggered myself.*	
Ways to demonstrate I am listening: *I have used some or all of the Active Listening techniques to show the other party (or parties) that I am listening.*	
Perception Check: *I have checked my perceptions and tested them to see if they correspond to reality.*	
Intent vs. impact: *I have synchronized the intent (motive or purpose) of the conversation and of any statements made to ensure the proper emotional impact.*	
Opening "I" Statement: *I have prepared an opening statement framed as something about me and my feelings or needs, rather than about them.*	
Fifth House Creative Conversation discussion points: *I have developed a list of discussion points that give us a helpful, mutually agreeable starting point for our problem-solving.*	

If you really want to increase your chances of having a successful conversation, the next worksheet is also well worth the time it takes to complete. Once again, like the other worksheets presented here, the Fifth House Creative Conversations Preparation Worksheet is available as a free download from the Fifth House Group website.

Fifth House Creative Conversations Preparation Worksheet

1. Gather the information:

What are your observations of the situation? What was said or done, and what were the circumstances? Stick to the actual words and actions heard and seen, and avoid making assumptions or attributing behaviours or causes. Include only the things that any neutral observer would agree to be true. (**Note**: use extra pages where required.)

2. Pause for self-reflection (be completely honest when describing the following):

- *What's important to me*: What need is being threatened or challenged here? What is it about this situation that is getting me anxious?
- *My attitude*: Am I entrenched in a position or being unnecessarily aggressive? Is this really about me being right and the other person being wrong? Am I truly interested in solving the problem together, or am I looking to score points? Am I avoiding the situation, hoping it will go away or get better on its own?
- *My hot buttons*: What are the things that trigger me? What words or actions readily cause me to feel insulted, defensive, or angry?
- *My emotions and how I might react*: What do I need to

do to make sure I don't get destructive?
- Does anyone else need to be involved in this conversation before decisions are made?

3. **Pause to reflect on the other person**:
   - What's important to him/her?
   - *Their attitude*: What can I do to make sure s/he feels as safe and comfortable as possible?
   - *Their hot buttons*: What are they? What can I do to make sure I don't pull any Conflict Escalation Triggers?
   - *Their emotions*: How might they react? What can I do to make sure I don't contribute to a negative reaction?

4. **Next steps**:
   - Review the Preparation Checklist.
   - Prepare to raise the issue and extend an invitation to the other person(s).
   - Prepare and suggest a date/time and the duration of

meeting.
- Determine the location (consider physical layout, comfort, discretion, neutrality, no distractions).

5. **Review the 5-step Fifth House Creative Conversations Model:**

    1. Tell each other your stories.

    2. Identify what you want to resolve.

    3. Develop options and potential solutions.

    4. Articulate agreement and set follow-up meeting.

    5. Hold follow-up meeting to ensure everything is working.

INDEX

www.ingramcontent.com/pod-product-compliance
Lightning Source LLC
LaVergne TN
LVHW021450080426
835509LV00018B/2232